Social Media Frauds and Online Scams

C. P. Kumar
Reiki Healer & Author
Roorkee - 247667, India

Copyright © 2024 C. P. Kumar

All rights reserved.

No part of this book may be reproduced or transmitted in any form or by any means, electronic or mechanical, including photocopying, recording, or by any information storage and retrieval system, without permission in writing from the author.

Disclaimer

While every effort has been made to ensure the accuracy and completeness of the content in this book, the author cannot guarantee that the information contained herein is error-free, up-to-date, or suitable for every individual circumstance.

The author shall not be held liable or responsible for any errors or omissions in the content of the book, nor for any damages, or losses that may arise from any actions taken based upon the suggestions or contents presented in the book.

Readers are advised to use their own judgment and discretion in applying the information provided in this book, and to consult with qualified professionals before taking any action based on the contents of this book. The author disclaims any and all liability or responsibility for any actions taken or not taken based on the information contained in this book.

DEDICATION

To all the individuals who have fallen victim to the shadows lurking in the corners of social media, this book is dedicated to your resilience and courage. To the tireless advocates, researchers, and cybersecurity professionals working to expose and combat online fraud - your relentless pursuit of justice inspires us all. May this work serve as a beacon of awareness, helping others navigate the complexities of the digital world with wisdom, caution, and strength.

C. P. Kumar

CONTENTS

Copyright 2
Disclaimer 3
DEDICATION 4
PREFACE 6
Chapter 1.   The Evolution of Social Media Scams 8
Chapter 2.   Privacy and Security Gaps 15
Chapter 3.   Data Harvesting 22
Chapter 4.   Fake Profiles 30
Chapter 5.   Account Takeover 37
Chapter 6.   Phishing Scams on Social Media 45
Chapter 7.   Romance Scams 52
Chapter 8.   Catfishing 60
Chapter 9.   Fraud through Impersonation 67
Chapter 10. Influencer Fraud 74
Chapter 11. AI-Driven Scams 81
Chapter 12. Fake Video Calls and Deepfakes 88
Chapter 13. Blackmail via Social Media 95
Chapter 14. The Rise of Fake Phone Calls 102
Chapter 15. Financial Scams and Cryptocurrency Fraud 109
Chapter 16. Social Media Ad Scams 117
Chapter 17. Marketplace Scams 124
Chapter 18. Combating Social Media Fraud 132
Other Books by the Author 139

PREFACE

In the digital age, social media has revolutionized the way we connect, communicate, and share our lives. However, alongside this evolution has come an alarming rise in online fraud, with scammers adapting swiftly to exploit the very platforms that were designed to bring people together. Social Media Frauds and Online Scams explores this dark undercurrent of the digital landscape, shedding light on the mechanisms and strategies employed by fraudsters who prey on unsuspecting users.

This book delves into the myriad ways in which social media platforms have inadvertently become a breeding ground for deception, manipulation, and theft. It uncovers the vulnerabilities within these platforms - gaps in privacy, security, and oversight - that have allowed fraud to thrive, and exposes the various techniques scammers use to harvest data, create false personas, and execute elaborate schemes that often have devastating financial and emotional consequences for their victims.

Throughout these pages, readers will gain a deeper understanding of how fraudsters manipulate social media, whether through phishing links, fake profiles, or even more advanced methods such as deepfakes and AI-driven scams. From romance fraud to cryptocurrency schemes, the tactics are diverse but share a common thread: the exploitation of trust. This book not only illuminates these dangers but also equips readers with knowledge and tools to navigate the social media minefield more safely.

The chapters that follow offer a comprehensive guide to the ever-evolving world of social media scams, encouraging vigilance and offering hope through awareness and preventive strategies. It is a call to action for individuals to protect themselves and a reminder of the importance of digital literacy in an increasingly connected but vulnerable world.

A list of my other published works on spiritual topics and social issues can be found at the end of this book. You may like to explore a few of my other books.

C. P. Kumar
Reiki Healer, Blogger & Author
Former Scientist 'G', National Institute of Hydrology
Roorkee - 247667, India
Web: https://www.angelfire.com/nh/cpkumar/virgo.html

Chapter 1. The Evolution of Social Media Scams

Introduction

The digital age has transformed the way humans interact, communicate, and conduct business. With the advent of social media platforms in the early 2000s, the potential for connectivity expanded exponentially. Social media, originally designed as a space to connect with friends, share updates, and engage with content, quickly evolved into a complex ecosystem of personal, professional, and commercial interactions. However, as the influence and reach of platforms like Facebook, Instagram, Twitter (X), and LinkedIn grew, so did the interest of malicious actors. What began as a few isolated incidents of hacking or minor scams has escalated into a global phenomenon where social media has become a hotbed for fraud. Scammers have adapted to the fast-paced and ever-changing environment of social media, developing sophisticated schemes that continue to evolve alongside technology and user behavior.

The Early Days: The Birth of Social Media and Fraud

When platforms like MySpace and Facebook emerged in the mid-2000s, they were primarily used by younger demographics for personal interaction. During this era, social media scams were relatively rudimentary and low in volume. Common scams involved the hacking of personal profiles to send out spammy messages or phishing links to friends. These early scams were less targeted and generally relied on the naivety of users unfamiliar with online threats. However, as social media networks grew, so did the realization of their immense potential for fraud.

As the number of social media users expanded into the billions, scammers recognized that these platforms provided unparalleled access to personal data and a direct communication line to unsuspecting users. The potential for anonymity on these platforms, combined with the massive user base, created a breeding ground for fraudulent schemes. By the early 2010s, social media fraud began taking on more organized and professional forms, setting the stage for increasingly sophisticated scams.

The Rise of Sophisticated Scams: 2010s and Beyond

As social media platforms started integrating with other digital services - such as online marketplaces, payment gateways, and advertising networks - the nature of scams began to evolve. The 2010s saw the rise of more complex and targeted fraud schemes that exploited the vulnerabilities in social media's infrastructure. Scammers started using tactics that mirrored the evolution of the platforms themselves: from catfishing and fake profiles to account takeovers and intricate phishing campaigns.

One of the defining characteristics of this period was the rise of 'social engineering' - a type of fraud where scammers manipulate users into divulging personal information, typically by posing as trusted contacts or authoritative figures. Social media, with its inherent trust-building mechanisms such as friend requests, followers, and personal messages, became the perfect breeding ground for these types of scams. Fraudsters could easily create fake profiles, clone accounts, and impersonate individuals or organizations with minimal risk of detection. This made social media an attractive playground for both petty criminals and organized crime syndicates alike.

The Growth of Marketplace and Financial Scams

As platforms like Facebook and Instagram introduced features allowing users to buy and sell goods, marketplace scams began to proliferate. Fraudsters would set up fake profiles to sell counterfeit or non-existent products, luring unsuspecting buyers with enticing deals. These types of scams capitalized on the rapid rise of e-commerce and social commerce, where users began to treat social media platforms not just as spaces for communication, but as marketplaces for goods and services.

In parallel, financial scams also flourished. With the introduction of digital payment systems and the growing popularity of cryptocurrencies, scammers took advantage of users' limited understanding of new financial technologies. Ponzi schemes, pyramid schemes, and fraudulent investment opportunities became rampant, particularly on platforms like Facebook and Twitter (X). Scammers would pose as successful investors or financial gurus, offering 'once-in-a-lifetime' opportunities that often promised quick and unrealistic returns. Many users, caught in the hype and trust of these platforms, fell victim to these schemes.

Social Media as a Tool for Identity Theft

One of the most significant turning points in the evolution of social media fraud was the increased use of platforms as a tool for identity theft. As users voluntarily shared more of their lives online - ranging from personal photos and status updates to location check-ins and professional details - scammers found it easier to harvest personal data that could be used to commit fraud.

In many cases, scammers would clone profiles or create fake accounts mimicking real users. These fake accounts could then be used to engage with the victim's friends and family, soliciting money under false pretenses or spreading malware through malicious links. The use of social media for identity theft has become so pervasive that it is now one of the leading causes of online fraud globally.

Moreover, the interconnected nature of social media means that once a victim's data is compromised on one platform, it can quickly spread to others. For example, a scammer who gains access to someone's Facebook account can often find enough information to compromise their email, bank account, or other social media profiles. This cross-platform vulnerability has made social media not only a target for scams but also a gateway to broader identity theft.

Phishing and Impersonation Scams

Phishing scams have long been a favorite tactic of online fraudsters, but the rise of social media has introduced new and more effective methods of phishing. Traditionally, phishing involved sending emails that appeared to be from trusted institutions like banks or government agencies. However, with social media, scammers can impersonate someone's friend, family member, or colleague, making phishing attempts far more believable.

A common scam involves fraudsters hacking into an account and sending messages to the victim's contacts, asking for help in the form of money or personal information. Because these messages appear to come from someone the victim knows and trusts, they are far more likely to fall for the scam. Additionally, with the growing use of mobile devices to access social media, users are often more susceptible to phishing attempts, as smaller screens and mobile interfaces can obscure telltale signs of a scam.

The Age of AI-Driven Scams and Deepfakes

As technology has advanced, so too have the tools available to scammers. Artificial intelligence (AI) has opened up new possibilities for social media fraud, particularly through the use of synthetic voices and deepfakes. AI-generated voices can be used to impersonate someone's voice with remarkable accuracy, making it easier for fraudsters to trick victims into believing they are speaking with a trusted friend or authority figure.

Deepfake technology, which allows for the creation of highly realistic but entirely fake videos, is another emerging threat. Fraudsters can now produce videos that appear to show someone - a celebrity, politician, or even a personal acquaintance - engaging in actions or making statements that they never actually did. These deepfakes can be used for blackmail, extortion, or to manipulate public opinion.

While the use of AI-driven scams and deepfakes is still in its early stages, their potential for harm is enormous. As this technology becomes more accessible and more convincing, it is likely to become a central tool in the arsenal of social media fraudsters.

The Globalization of Social Media Scams

One of the defining features of social media fraud is its global nature. Social media platforms connect users from all over the world, which means that scammers can target victims in multiple countries simultaneously. This globalization has made it difficult for law enforcement agencies to combat social media fraud, as scammers often operate across international borders, making it harder to track and prosecute them.

Moreover, the sheer scale of social media platforms means that even if a scam is detected, it can spread to millions of users before it is stopped. Platforms like Facebook and Instagram have introduced measures to detect and prevent fraud, but these efforts often lag behind the constantly evolving tactics of scammers.

In developing countries, where social media usage is growing rapidly, users are often more vulnerable to scams due to lower levels of digital literacy and less access to information about online fraud. Scammers have taken advantage of this, targeting users in regions where social media is a relatively new phenomenon and where regulatory frameworks to protect users are still underdeveloped.

Conclusion: A Constantly Evolving Threat

The evolution of social media scams reflects the broader trends of the digital age: as technology advances, so too do the tactics of fraudsters. What started as simple account hacks and phishing attempts has grown into a complex web of deception that spans platforms, borders, and technologies. Social media has become not just a tool for communication, but a battleground where users must remain vigilant against ever-evolving threats. As AI and deepfake technology become more prevalent, the line between reality and deception on social media is becoming increasingly blurred, and users must adapt their defenses accordingly.

In the chapters that follow, we will explore in greater detail the various tactics scammers use, from data harvesting and fake profiles to AI-driven scams and deepfakes. Understanding these threats is the first step toward protecting oneself in the digital age. Social media may have revolutionized the way we interact, but it has also opened up new vulnerabilities that we must confront head-on.

Chapter 2. Privacy and Security Gaps
How Platforms Enable Scams

Introduction

In the age of social media dominance, platforms like Facebook, Instagram, and Twitter (X) have become integral parts of our daily lives. They allow us to connect, share, and interact with individuals from all corners of the world, presenting a dynamic ecosystem of content, commerce, and communication. However, while these platforms offer vast potential for personal and business growth, they also present significant risks. A concerning number of scams, frauds, and malicious activities exploit the very features that make social media so attractive. In this chapter, we will examine the privacy and security gaps that these platforms harbor and explore how these vulnerabilities enable scammers to operate with impunity.

The Nature of Social Media: Open and Accessible

One of the primary reasons social media platforms are vulnerable to exploitation is their open and accessible nature. Facebook and Instagram, for instance, encourage users to connect with new people, share updates about their lives, and explore an array of multimedia content. This openness is foundational to the user experience, making these platforms appealing not only for social interactions but also for brands, advertisers, and content creators. However, this same openness makes it easier for scammers to blend in with legitimate users, posing as friends, brands, or influencers.

Scammers exploit the trust that users naturally build within their networks. Often, they create fake profiles or hijack existing ones to impersonate people or entities. For instance, a fraudster may create a profile that mimics a popular brand or public figure, luring users into giveaways or investment schemes that are designed to steal personal information or money. The nature of social media, which promotes quick and superficial connections, makes it difficult for users to vet these connections properly. As a result, even well-educated individuals can fall prey to scams disguised as legitimate opportunities or friendships.

Weak Identity Verification and Oversight

A significant privacy and security gap in platforms like Facebook and Instagram is the lack of stringent identity verification processes. While users are required to provide basic information such as an email address and phone number, these details are easy to falsify or manipulate. Scammers frequently exploit this loophole, creating multiple fake accounts to carry out their fraudulent activities without facing immediate repercussions.

The sheer volume of users on these platforms makes it challenging for moderation teams to detect and disable fake profiles in real-time. This reactive approach - waiting for users to report suspicious activity - often means that scammers can operate for weeks or even months before they are flagged and removed. During this time, they can victimize hundreds or even thousands of people. The absence of robust identity verification measures allows fraudsters to bypass detection, creating an environment where the digital identity of a user can be easily manipulated.

In addition to identity verification challenges, the problem is compounded by the platforms' own algorithmic designs. Algorithms prioritize engagement, meaning that posts that generate high levels of interaction, such as likes, shares, and comments, are more likely to be promoted to a broader audience. Scammers take advantage of this by creating content designed to spark curiosity, fear, or urgency - classic techniques for pulling users into fraudulent schemes. The platforms' automated systems amplify the reach of these scams before human moderators can intervene.

Exploiting the Advertising Systems

Social media platforms have transformed how businesses and individuals advertise their products and services. While this democratization of advertising is beneficial for many small businesses and creators, it also presents opportunities for scammers. Platforms like Facebook and Instagram rely heavily on targeted advertising models that use user data to match advertisers with specific audiences. Unfortunately, the advertising system itself can be easily manipulated by fraudsters who wish to exploit its reach and influence.

Scammers can purchase ads that appear legitimate but lead users to fraudulent websites or offers. For example, they may create an ad for an incredibly cheap product that redirects users to a phishing site designed to steal credit card information. While platforms have mechanisms for detecting malicious ads, these systems are far from perfect. The volume of ads being served at any given time is staggering, and fraudsters often employ tactics like rapidly changing their domains or altering the content of the ad to avoid detection.

Additionally, the anonymity afforded by these platforms enables scammers to remain faceless and untraceable. Advertising accounts can be created with little verification, and scammers can disappear with the stolen money long before any investigation or action takes place. This lack of accountability makes social media platforms a prime avenue for financial fraud and scams that target vulnerable users.

Inadequate Data Privacy Protections

Data privacy has become a critical issue in recent years, with numerous high-profile breaches and scandals highlighting how vulnerable personal information can be on social media platforms. Facebook's Cambridge Analytica scandal in 2018 demonstrated how data harvested from users could be weaponized to manipulate elections and undermine public trust. However, the misuse of personal data extends far beyond political campaigns. Scammers also exploit these vulnerabilities to target individuals for various fraudulent schemes.

Many social media platforms collect vast amounts of data on their users, including location information, browsing habits, interests, and even offline behavior. This data, often used to improve user experience and deliver targeted ads, is also a goldmine for fraudsters. With access to detailed profiles, scammers can craft highly convincing schemes tailored to the interests and behaviors of their victims. For example, a scammer might target a user who frequently posts about fitness with a fraudulent offer for a discounted gym membership, complete with a professional-looking website and testimonials from fake users.

Moreover, the opaque privacy policies of many platforms leave users unaware of how their data is being used or shared. This lack of transparency is a significant security gap, as it leaves individuals vulnerable to data misuse without their explicit knowledge. Once data is harvested by scammers, whether through phishing attacks, data breaches, or malicious apps, it can be sold on the dark web or used to launch more sophisticated fraud campaigns.

Phishing Scams and Social Engineering

Phishing is one of the most common scams on social media platforms, and it thrives due to the inherent trust that users place in their social connections. A phishing attack typically involves a scammer sending a message or email that appears to come from a trusted source, such as a friend or a brand. These messages often contain a sense of urgency, prompting the recipient to click on a link or provide personal information. Once the user complies, their data is either stolen or used to further propagate the scam.

Social media platforms are particularly vulnerable to phishing because of the casual and conversational nature of interactions. Scammers may hijack a legitimate account and send phishing messages to all of the victim's contacts, making it more likely that the message will be trusted. Alternatively, they may create fake accounts that mimic those of trusted individuals or companies, further enhancing the credibility of their phishing attempts.

Social engineering attacks, where scammers manipulate users into revealing confidential information, are also prevalent on social media. These attacks often involve building a relationship with the victim over time, earning their trust before asking for sensitive information such as passwords or financial details. The personal nature of social media makes it an ideal breeding ground for these types of scams, as users are more likely to let their guard down in what they perceive as a familiar and safe environment.

Impersonation and Account Hijacking

Impersonation and account hijacking are two of the most damaging tactics used by scammers on social media platforms. In impersonation scams, fraudsters create fake profiles that closely mimic the profiles of real people or brands. They may steal profile pictures, bios, and even past posts to make the account look legitimate. Once the fake profile is established, the scammer can reach out to the victim's friends, family, or followers, asking for money or personal information under the guise of a trusted individual.

Account hijacking, on the other hand, involves taking over an existing account, often through phishing or weak password security. Once a scammer gains access to an account, they can wreak havoc by posting malicious content, sending fraudulent messages, or stealing sensitive information stored in private messages. In some cases, scammers will demand a ransom from the victim in exchange for returning control of the account.

Both impersonation and account hijacking are facilitated by the fact that social media platforms often have inadequate security features. Two-factor authentication, while available on most major platforms, is not always enforced or used by users. Additionally, password recovery systems can be exploited by scammers who gain access to an email or phone number associated with the account. The consequences of these attacks can be devastating, leading to financial loss, reputational damage, and emotional distress for victims.

The Role of Platform Policies and User Responsibility

While social media platforms have made strides in improving security and privacy measures, there is still much work to be done. Platforms must strike a delicate balance between providing an open and engaging user experience and protecting their users from malicious actors. This requires stronger identity verification measures, more robust algorithms for detecting fraudulent activity, and greater transparency around data privacy practices.

At the same time, users must also take responsibility for their own security. Simple steps like enabling two-factor authentication, using strong and unique passwords, and being cautious about the information shared online can go a long way in protecting against scams. Education and awareness are crucial components in the fight against social media fraud, as many users are simply unaware of the risks they face.

Conclusion

The privacy and security gaps in social media platforms like Facebook and Instagram create an environment where scams and fraud can flourish. Weak identity verification, inadequate data privacy protections, and the exploitation of advertising systems all contribute to the problem. However, through concerted efforts from both platforms and users, these vulnerabilities can be addressed, creating a safer and more secure social media landscape for everyone.

Chapter 3. Data Harvesting
How Scammers Mine Information

Introduction

In an era where the internet has become an integral part of daily life, social media platforms serve as a central hub for communication, networking, and sharing personal experiences. While these platforms are designed to connect people, they have also become fertile ground for malicious actors seeking to harvest personal data for fraudulent purposes. Data harvesting refers to the large-scale collection of personal information from various sources, often done without the user's knowledge or consent. This practice is particularly pervasive on social media, where users voluntarily share details of their lives, creating a goldmine for scammers.

Scammers exploit the vast amounts of information available on social media, from personal details to behavioral patterns, to commit a range of fraudulent activities. In this article, we will explore how data harvesting works, the techniques scammers use to mine personal information, and the devastating impacts these scams can have on individuals and society.

The Allure of Social Media for Scammers

Social media platforms have transformed the way people communicate and present themselves to the world. Platforms like Facebook, Instagram, Twitter (X), and LinkedIn encourage users to share snippets of their personal lives, professional achievements, and interests. These details are publicly accessible unless users specifically adjust their privacy settings, which many often neglect.

Scammers see social media as a treasure trove of personal data because the information users share can reveal much more than what they intend. Names, birthdates, addresses, phone numbers, and employment details are often openly shared, either directly or through context clues in posts. Even seemingly innocuous information such as likes, interests, and location check-ins can be used by scammers to build a comprehensive profile of an individual.

The global reach and popularity of social media also make it an appealing target for scammers. Millions of people share content every day, giving malicious actors a constant stream of fresh data to harvest. Moreover, social media's interactive nature - through comments, likes, and messages - gives scammers additional channels to gather personal information through phishing, impersonation, and manipulation.

Techniques Scammers Use to Harvest Data

Scammers employ a variety of tactics to collect personal information from social media users. These techniques range from sophisticated hacking methods to more straightforward social engineering tricks. Below are some of the most common methods used by scammers to mine information from unsuspecting users.

1. Phishing Attacks

Phishing is one of the oldest and most effective tactics used by scammers to trick users into providing personal information. On social media, phishing usually takes the form of fake messages, emails, or websites that mimic legitimate platforms. Scammers often send direct messages to users, posing as friends, colleagues, or even the social media platform itself, asking for login credentials or personal information. They may use enticing messages such as "You've won a prize!" or "There's a problem with your account, please update your information."

Once the user falls for the bait and provides the requested information, scammers can gain access to their account and extract further details. Phishing attacks can also involve fake login pages that capture usernames and passwords, allowing scammers to hijack accounts for future scams.

2. Fake Profiles and Impersonation

Creating fake profiles is another common tactic scammers use to collect personal information. Scammers may create fake profiles that appear to be legitimate businesses, celebrities, or even friends of the user. They then engage with users to build trust before asking for personal information.

Impersonation is a variation of this tactic, where scammers hack into an existing account and pose as the original account holder. Friends and family of the hacked individual may be targeted, as they are more likely to trust messages coming from someone they know. Scammers can use this trust to ask for money, personal information, or access to sensitive accounts.

3. Quizzes and Surveys

Online quizzes and surveys are ubiquitous on social media, often promising fun results like "Which celebrity are you most like?" or "What's your spirit animal?" While many users take these quizzes for entertainment, scammers use them as tools to gather information.

These quizzes often ask questions that may seem harmless but are designed to extract personal details. For example, questions about favorite foods, childhood memories, or pet names can actually be used to guess security questions for online accounts. Additionally, many quizzes require users to grant access to their social media profiles, which allows scammers to harvest even more data from their accounts, including friends lists, photos, and contact details.

4. Data Scraping

Data scraping refers to the automated extraction of publicly available information from websites and social media platforms. Scammers use software tools called scrapers to mine data from users' profiles, posts, comments, and other public information.

While some scraping activities are legal, such as when companies use scraping tools for market research, scammers use it for malicious purposes. For instance, scammers may scrape public profiles for email addresses, phone numbers, and other contact information, which can later be used for spam, phishing, or identity theft.

Scraping tools can also collect information on a user's behavior, such as their interests, interactions, and locations. This behavioral data allows scammers to craft more convincing phishing attacks and social engineering tactics, as they can tailor their messages to appear more personalized and legitimate.

5. Malware and Keyloggers

In more technical attacks, scammers use malware and keyloggers to harvest personal information. Malware can be introduced to a user's device through links shared on social media, often disguised as videos, downloads, or exclusive content. Once the user clicks on the link, the malware is installed, giving the scammer access to the user's device, social media accounts, and any stored personal information.

Keyloggers are a type of malware that records every keystroke made on a device. Scammers use keyloggers to capture login credentials, private messages, and other sensitive information typed by the user. Once the scammer has access to this data, they can hijack accounts, steal identities, or commit financial fraud.

6. Friend Requests and Direct Messages

A more straightforward method of data harvesting involves sending friend requests or direct messages to unsuspecting users. Scammers may pose as new acquaintances, colleagues, or friends of friends to gain access to a user's profile. Once the connection is established, scammers can view more personal information that may not be visible to the public, such as email addresses, phone numbers, and private posts.

Direct messages also provide scammers with an opportunity to engage users in conversation, often leading to phishing or social engineering tactics. Scammers may ask for personal details directly, or manipulate the conversation to extract information subtly.

How Scammers Exploit Harvested Data

The data that scammers harvest from social media can be used in a variety of fraudulent activities. Below are some of the ways in which harvested data is exploited.

1. Identity Theft

One of the most common uses of harvested data is identity theft. Scammers can use personal information such as names, birthdates, and addresses to impersonate individuals and open credit cards, take out loans, or commit other financial fraud. Once a scammer has enough details, they can easily assume the identity of the victim, leading to severe financial and emotional distress for the affected individuals.

2. Account Takeovers

With access to login credentials obtained through phishing or other means, scammers can take over social media accounts and use them for further fraud. Once an account is hijacked, scammers can send messages to the victim's contacts, asking for money or personal information. These account takeovers can also be used to spread malware or promote fraudulent schemes to a broader audience.

3. Financial Fraud

Scammers often use harvested data to commit financial fraud, such as draining bank accounts or making unauthorized purchases. They may also use the information to create fake identities, which can be used to apply for loans, credit cards, or government benefits.

In some cases, scammers may sell harvested data on the dark web, where other criminals purchase the information to commit their own fraudulent activities. The financial consequences of these actions can be devastating for victims, who may be left dealing with the fallout for years.

4. Social Engineering Attacks

Scammers use the data they collect to craft convincing social engineering attacks, where they manipulate individuals into divulging more information or taking specific actions. For example, a scammer may use details about a victim's job or personal life to pose as a colleague or friend and ask for sensitive information. These attacks are often successful because they are tailored to the victim's unique circumstances, making them harder to detect.

Protecting Yourself from Data Harvesting

While social media offers a convenient way to stay connected with others, it's essential to be vigilant about the information you share. To protect yourself from data harvesting, consider the following steps:

Adjust Privacy Settings: Ensure your social media accounts are set to private, so only trusted friends and family can see your personal information.

Be Selective About Sharing: Avoid posting sensitive information such as your home address, phone number, or financial details.

Watch for Phishing Scams: Be cautious of messages and emails asking for personal information, especially if they seem urgent or too good to be true.

Limit Third-Party Access: Be wary of quizzes, surveys, and apps that request access to your social media profile, as they may be collecting more information than necessary.

Use Strong Passwords: Ensure your social media accounts are protected with strong, unique passwords, and enable two-factor authentication for added security.

Conclusion

Data harvesting on social media is a growing threat that can have severe consequences for individuals and society. By understanding the tactics scammers use and taking proactive measures to protect personal information, users can reduce their risk of falling victim to these scams. As social media continues to evolve, staying informed and vigilant will remain essential in the fight against online fraud and data exploitation.

Chapter 4. Fake Profiles
The Art of Deception

Introduction

In the modern digital age, social media platforms have become an essential part of everyday life. They allow people to connect, share, and communicate across the globe. However, with this increased connectivity comes the dark side of the online world - fraud and scams. One of the most prevalent tactics used by scammers today is the creation of fake profiles. These deceptive personas allow fraudsters to manipulate, deceive, and victimize unsuspecting users. The art of creating and maintaining fake profiles is a fundamental weapon in the arsenal of online scammers. This article delves into the intricacies of how fake profiles are created, the various tactics scammers use to establish credibility, and the potential dangers they pose to innocent users.

The Foundation of a Fake Profile

At the heart of many online scams lies a fake profile - a carefully curated digital persona designed to appear legitimate, trustworthy, and appealing to its target audience. The construction of a fake profile is often a calculated process, where scammers piece together information, photos, and personal details to mimic a real person. These profiles can range from fake celebrities to false business entities, and even fabricated romantic interests.

The process typically begins with the creation of a name and background story. Scammers will often use names that sound common and credible, or names similar to those of well-known individuals to build immediate trust. This can also include stolen personal information from real people to further the illusion. With the name comes a backstory that makes the profile appear believable, such as a job, education history, or a location that aligns with the platform's demographics.

The next step involves the selection of profile pictures. Scammers will often steal photos from real users, celebrities, or stock images, and pass them off as their own. The goal is to make the profile appear visually appealing and credible, further enhancing the sense of legitimacy. Scammers may also enhance their profiles by adding fake interests, hobbies, and content that aligns with the persona they want to project, giving the illusion of an active and real user.

Establishing Credibility: The Trust-Building Phase

One of the most critical steps in the art of deception through fake profiles is the trust-building phase. Scammers understand that in order to execute their fraudulent schemes successfully, they must first establish credibility with their targets. This trust-building process can take days, weeks, or even months, depending on the complexity of the scam and the nature of the target.

Scammers use various tactics to gain trust. They may engage with the target in conversation, share posts that reflect shared interests, or interact with mutual acquaintances to seem more connected. Some scammers even go to the extent of building networks of fake profiles that interact with each other, creating an elaborate web of deceit that gives the impression of authenticity.

In online dating scams, for example, the scammer may slowly develop a relationship with the victim, showing affection, understanding, and empathy to establish an emotional connection. This emotional manipulation is designed to make the victim vulnerable and more likely to fall prey to the scam later on. Similarly, in business-related scams, a fake profile might represent a successful entrepreneur or businessperson offering an exciting investment opportunity. By showcasing a luxurious lifestyle, posting about their "success", or sharing fabricated testimonials from other fake profiles, they create a false sense of credibility.

Types of Fake Profiles and Their Motivations

Fake profiles can serve various purposes, each tailored to a different type of scam. Understanding the different types of fake profiles and the motivation behind them helps in identifying potential red flags and protecting oneself from falling victim.

1. Romantic Fake Profiles: These are common in online dating scams, where scammers create fake personas to woo and seduce their targets emotionally. The motivation behind these profiles is usually financial gain, as scammers typically ask for money after gaining the victim's trust by pretending to need funds for emergencies or to visit the victim in person. Romance scams are particularly devastating as they exploit the victim's emotional vulnerability, often leading to significant financial loss.

2. Business or Professional Fake Profiles: **Scammers posing as professionals or business entities create fake profiles to lure victims into fraudulent business deals or investments. They often present themselves as successful entrepreneurs, CEOs, or high-ranking officials, offering "too good to be true" investment opportunities. In some cases, these fake profiles may even offer job opportunities to unsuspecting

individuals, asking for personal information or payment to secure the position.

3. Celebrity Impersonators: **Many scammers create fake profiles mimicking celebrities or public figures.** They may use these fake profiles to promote fraudulent products or services, or even to ask for donations for fake charitable causes. Fans of these celebrities are often targeted, as their admiration for the public figure may cloud their judgment and make them more susceptible to manipulation.

4. Social Media Influencers: **As influencer culture grows on platforms like Instagram and TikTok, scammers have started creating fake influencer profiles to promote counterfeit goods or services.** These fake influencers may advertise products that never get delivered or are of poor quality, leaving victims without their money or the promised goods.

5. Government Official Impersonators: **Some scammers create fake profiles posing as government officials or law enforcement officers.** They use these profiles to intimidate victims, often claiming that the victim is under investigation or owes money to the government. The scammer then demands payment to "resolve" the issue, preying on the victim's fear of legal consequences.

The Psychology Behind the Scam

The success of fake profiles largely depends on the psychological manipulation of the target. Scammers exploit various psychological triggers to make their deception more effective. One common tactic is to appeal to the victim's emotions, whether it's by creating an emotional bond in romance scams or by playing on fear in government impersonation scams. Scammers also take advantage of the scarcity principle by presenting their fraudulent opportunities as limited-time offers or once-in-a-lifetime chances, pushing victims to act quickly without thinking critically.

Another psychological tool is social proof. By creating networks of fake profiles that interact with each other, scammers simulate a community or network of people who support the fake persona. This gives the impression that the profile is legitimate, as other "users" seem to vouch for its credibility. Victims are less likely to question the authenticity of a profile when they see others engaging with it positively.

Finally, scammers rely on the innate human tendency to trust. Most social media users assume that the people they interact with online are real and trustworthy, especially when their profiles appear genuine. Scammers exploit this trust to their advantage, knowing that few people will investigate the legitimacy of a profile before engaging with it.

The Impact on Victims

The consequences of falling victim to a fake profile can be devastating. Financial loss is one of the most common outcomes, particularly in romance or business-related scams. Victims may be tricked into sending large sums of money to scammers, believing they are helping someone in need or investing in a legitimate business opportunity. In some cases, victims may even take out loans or deplete their savings to support the scammer.

Emotional and psychological damage is another significant impact. Victims of romance scams, in particular, often suffer from feelings of betrayal, embarrassment, and shame after realizing they have been deceived. The emotional manipulation that scammers use to gain trust can leave deep scars, making it difficult for victims to trust others in the future.

In addition to financial and emotional harm, victims may also face reputational damage. Scammers often use victims' personal information to create additional fake profiles, perpetuating the cycle of fraud. This can result in the victim's name being associated with scams or fraudulent activities, tarnishing their online reputation.

How to Protect Yourself from Fake Profiles

While the dangers of fake profiles are real, there are steps that social media users can take to protect themselves from falling victim to these scams. First and foremost, it's essential to remain vigilant and skeptical of profiles that seem too good to be true. Always verify the identity of someone before engaging in personal or financial transactions. This can be done by conducting a reverse image search of their profile picture, looking for inconsistencies in their backstory, or cross-referencing their information with other sources.

Be cautious of profiles that seem overly eager to establish a relationship or business deal. Scammers often rush the trust-building process to manipulate their victims quickly. If someone you barely know is asking for money, personal information, or other forms of assistance, it's a major red flag.

Lastly, report suspicious profiles to the platform's administration. Social media platforms have mechanisms in place to investigate and remove fake profiles. By reporting a fake profile, you not only protect yourself but also help prevent others from falling victim to the same scam.

Conclusion

Fake profiles are a cornerstone of online fraud and deception. They allow scammers to craft personas that manipulate, deceive, and victimize unsuspecting social media users. By understanding the tactics behind the creation of fake profiles and remaining vigilant, users can protect themselves from falling prey to these sophisticated scams. While technology continues to evolve, the human element of trust and connection remains at the core of online interactions - making it more important than ever to exercise caution in the digital world.

Chapter 5. Account Takeover
The Rise of Hacked Profiles

Introduction

In the interconnected world of social media, where millions share their daily lives, thoughts, and personal details, a sinister trend is on the rise - the takeover of personal accounts by fraudsters. The term "Account Takeover" (ATO) refers to when a cybercriminal gains unauthorized access to an individual's social media account and uses it to carry out malicious activities. These activities range from scamming the account owner's friends and followers to using the hacked profile as a tool for larger fraudulent schemes. As social media becomes more integrated into daily life, understanding how these takeovers happen and the dangers they pose is essential to safeguarding personal and online identities.

The Mechanics of Account Takeover

Account takeover is not a new phenomenon, but its scale and sophistication have evolved dramatically with the growing ubiquity of social media. At its core, an account takeover involves a fraudster gaining control of a user's social media profile by acquiring their login credentials, typically through deceptive means.

1. Phishing Attacks

One of the most common methods hackers use to obtain account credentials is phishing. Phishing attacks involve sending fraudulent messages designed to trick individuals into providing personal information, such as usernames, passwords, or credit card details. These messages often appear to come from a legitimate source, such as the social media platform itself, a friend, or a well-known company. For example, users might receive a message warning them that their account has been compromised and requesting they log in through a provided link. This link, however, directs them to a fake login page controlled by the fraudster, allowing the hacker to capture the user's credentials.

2. Brute Force Attacks

In a brute force attack, hackers attempt to gain access to accounts by systematically trying every possible combination of characters until they guess the correct password. While this method may sound time-consuming, the process has been streamlined through automated software that can test thousands of potential passwords in a short amount of time. Social media accounts with weak or common passwords (like "123456" or "password") are particularly vulnerable to brute force attacks. Once hackers obtain the correct password, they gain full control of the account.

3. Credential Stuffing

Credential stuffing is another method employed by hackers to take over social media accounts. This tactic involves using login credentials obtained from data breaches on one platform to access accounts on other platforms. For example, if a user's email and password are leaked in a breach of an online shopping site, and they use the same credentials for their social media accounts, hackers can use this information to log in to those accounts. Given that many individuals reuse passwords across multiple services, credential stuffing has become a highly effective technique for fraudsters.

4. Social Engineering

Social engineering refers to manipulating individuals into revealing confidential information. Fraudsters often exploit human trust and curiosity to gain access to social media accounts. They might pose as a trusted friend, colleague, or even a tech support representative from the social media platform itself, convincing users to share their login credentials. In some cases, hackers may impersonate the account owner's contacts and ask for personal details, which can be used to answer security questions or bypass two-factor authentication measures.

The Motivations Behind Account Takeover

Once a fraudster has control of a social media account, their motivations can vary, but they typically fall into a few broad categories. Understanding these motivations helps highlight the scope of damage a hacked profile can cause, not only to the account owner but to their friends, family, and followers as well.

1. Scamming Friends and Followers

One of the primary uses of a hijacked social media account is to scam the victim's friends and followers. Since the account appears to belong to someone they trust, people are more likely to fall for fraudulent schemes. Hackers may send messages asking for money, claiming the account owner is in urgent need or has encountered an emergency. In some cases, they may promote fake investment opportunities or online deals, enticing people to send money or provide sensitive information, believing the offer is legitimate. These scams are often successful because the victim's contacts trust the source of the message.

2. Spreading Malware

Social media accounts are a powerful vector for distributing malware. Hackers may send malicious links through direct messages or posts, often disguised as a video or photo that piques the recipient's curiosity. Clicking on these links can install malware on the victim's device, giving the hacker access to personal files, banking information, and more. Sometimes, the malware can be used to spread to other contacts, creating a cascading effect that amplifies the impact of the initial hack.

3. Identity Theft and Data Harvesting

Once fraudsters take over a social media account, they can access a wealth of personal information. This includes not only publicly visible data such as photos and posts but also private messages, email addresses, phone numbers, and connections to other accounts. This information can be used for identity theft or sold on the dark web to other criminals. For instance, the hacker might steal the victim's identity to open bank accounts, apply for loans, or commit other financial fraud. The more information available on the social media account, the greater the risk of identity theft.

4. Selling Accounts on the Dark Web

Another lucrative motive behind account takeovers is selling the hacked accounts on the dark web. Social media accounts, particularly those with large followings or verified status, are highly valuable to fraudsters. These accounts can be used for various malicious purposes, including running spam campaigns, promoting fake products, or even launching misinformation campaigns. A thriving black market exists for compromised social media profiles, and the more influential the account, the higher the price it commands.

The Impact on Victims

For the victims of account takeovers, the consequences can be far-reaching. Beyond the immediate loss of access to their accounts, victims may face reputational damage, financial loss, and emotional distress.

1. Reputational Damage

When a social media account is taken over, the hacker can post anything under the victim's name. Offensive posts, scams, and false information can quickly tarnish a person's reputation, both personally and professionally. In cases where business or public figures are targeted, the damage to their brand can be even more significant. The time and effort required to rebuild trust with friends, followers, and business connections can be overwhelming.

2. Financial Loss

Victims of account takeovers may suffer financially if the hacker uses their account to solicit money from friends or engage in fraudulent activities. In some cases, victims are extorted for money in exchange for the return of their account. Additionally, if the hacker accesses other connected accounts, such as online banking or e-commerce profiles, the financial losses can be devastating.

3. Emotional Distress

The emotional toll of an account takeover can be profound. Many victims feel violated and helpless as they watch their online identity being misused. The process of regaining control of the account can be stressful and time-consuming, especially if the social media platform's support team is slow to respond. The fear that personal information may be permanently compromised adds to the emotional strain.

Preventing Account Takeover

While the threat of account takeovers is real and growing, there are steps individuals can take to protect their social media profiles from being compromised.

1. Use Strong, Unique Passwords

A strong password is the first line of defense against account takeover. Users should avoid using easily guessable passwords, such as birthdays, names, or common phrases. Instead, they should opt for complex passwords that include a combination of letters, numbers, and symbols. It is also crucial to use different passwords for different accounts. Using a password manager can help users keep track of their various passwords securely.

2. Enable Two-Factor Authentication (2FA)

Two-factor authentication adds an extra layer of security by requiring users to verify their identity with a second method, such as a text message or authentication app. Even if a hacker manages to obtain a user's password, they will not be able to access the account without the second authentication factor. Enabling 2FA on social media accounts is one of the most effective ways to prevent account takeover.

3. Be Wary of Phishing Attempts

Users should be cautious when clicking on links or providing personal information in response to unsolicited messages, even if they appear to come from a trusted source. Before clicking on a link, it's important to verify the sender's identity and ensure the URL directs to a legitimate site. Social media platforms will never ask users to provide their login credentials through email or direct message.

4. Monitor Account Activity

Regularly monitoring account activity can help users spot signs of a potential takeover early. Many social media platforms allow users to review recent login locations and devices. If an unfamiliar device is listed, users should immediately change their password and log out of all devices. Additionally, enabling notifications for suspicious login attempts can provide real-time alerts if someone is trying to access the account.

5. Limit the Amount of Personal Information Shared

The less personal information available on social media profiles, the harder it is for hackers to exploit. Users should review their privacy settings and limit who can view sensitive details such as their email address, phone number, or date of birth. While sharing personal updates is a core part of social media, it's important to strike a balance between sharing and protecting personal privacy.

Conclusion

Account takeover is a growing threat in the digital age, and social media users must be vigilant to protect themselves from falling victim to these scams. Hackers employ a variety of tactics to gain control of accounts, and once they do, the consequences can be far-reaching. From scamming friends to spreading malware, the misuse of a hacked profile can cause financial, emotional, and reputational harm. However, by following best practices such as using strong passwords, enabling two-factor authentication, and being cautious of phishing attempts, individuals can significantly reduce their risk of becoming the next victim of an account takeover. In a world where our digital identities are increasingly intertwined with our personal and professional lives, taking steps to safeguard social media accounts has never been more important.

Chapter 6. Phishing Scams on Social Media
Beware of Clicks and Links

Introduction

In today's digitally connected world, social media has become an integral part of our lives. With millions of users engaging daily on platforms such as Facebook, Instagram, Twitter (X), LinkedIn, and TikTok, the opportunities for communication, networking, and sharing content are limitless. However, with the rise of social media, we have also seen an increase in fraudulent activities, particularly phishing scams. Phishing scams on social media present a significant threat to users' security, often appearing as innocent links, messages, or friend requests. These scams aim to steal sensitive information such as login credentials, credit card details, and other personal data.

This article explores the growing phenomenon of phishing scams on social media, how these scams work, and how you can protect yourself from falling victim to them.

The Nature of Phishing Scams on Social Media

Phishing is a type of online scam where fraudsters impersonate legitimate entities or individuals to trick users into sharing sensitive information. Traditionally, phishing scams were most common via email, but in recent years, cybercriminals have turned their attention to social media platforms. The growing popularity of social media has created a fertile ground for these scammers to exploit the trust users place in their online connections.

Social media phishing scams typically work by sending a user a message or link that appears legitimate. It could be from a fake profile posing as a friend, family member, or even a well-known organization. The message often contains an enticing call to action - such as claiming the user has won a prize, needs to verify account details, or is about to miss out on a limited-time offer. When the user clicks the link, they are taken to a fraudulent website that looks strikingly similar to the real one, where they are asked to provide sensitive information. Once the user submits this information, the scammers use it for malicious purposes, including identity theft and financial fraud.

Social Engineering: The Tactic Behind Phishing Scams

Phishing scams heavily rely on social engineering, a psychological manipulation technique that exploits human emotions such as fear, curiosity, and greed. Scammers craft their messages and fake profiles to appear as authentic and trustworthy as possible, often mimicking the tone and style of official communication. They also create a sense of urgency to pressure the victim into clicking on the link or providing information without thinking.

For instance, a phishing message might claim that your social media account has been hacked, and you need to reset your password immediately. The accompanying link leads to a fake login page that captures your username and password when entered. Another common tactic is to send a direct message or private message from a hacked friend's account, asking for help or money. Since the request seems to come from someone you trust, you are more likely to act without questioning its legitimacy.

Social media platforms are designed to encourage trust and sharing among users, making them especially vulnerable to social engineering tactics. The ability to forge a convincing identity and interact directly with potential victims makes phishing attacks particularly effective in this environment.

Common Types of Phishing Scams on Social Media

Phishing scams on social media come in many forms, and scammers are constantly evolving their tactics to bypass security measures. Some of the most common types of phishing scams that users should be aware of include:

1. Fake Account Scams

One of the most prevalent forms of phishing on social media involves creating fake profiles that impersonate real people, celebrities, or organizations. Scammers may create a profile that looks exactly like a friend, family member, or popular brand, complete with stolen profile pictures and similar usernames. They then send connection requests or direct messages to the victim, encouraging them to click on a malicious link or download harmful content.

These fake accounts often promise rewards or urge users to verify their information to gain access to exclusive content. Once users provide their login credentials or other personal details, scammers can gain unauthorized access to their real accounts, which can then be used to launch further attacks.

2. Message-Based Phishing (Smishing)

Message-based phishing, also known as "smishing" when conducted via SMS, involves sending fraudulent messages to a user's inbox on social media. These messages typically appear to come from a legitimate source, such as a trusted brand, online service, or even a friend. The message might claim that the user has won a prize, received a security alert, or is being asked to verify their account information.

The message usually contains a link that, when clicked, takes the user to a fake website designed to look like a legitimate login or payment page. By entering their details, users unknowingly provide scammers with access to their accounts, financial information, or personal data.

3. Giveaway Scams

Giveaway scams are a common type of phishing attack on platforms like Instagram and Facebook. Scammers create fake profiles posing as well-known brands or influencers and announce fake giveaways of expensive products like smartphones, luxury goods, or cash. These posts often go viral, spreading quickly as users are encouraged to share the post or tag friends to enter the contest.

To claim their "prize", users are typically asked to click on a link and provide personal information or credit card details for "shipping fees". In reality, the scammers collect this information for malicious purposes, leaving the user without the promised prize and potentially compromising their security.

4. Friend Requests from Hacked Accounts

Another popular phishing tactic involves taking over a legitimate user's social media account and using it to send friend requests or direct messages to their contacts. Since the request comes from a trusted source, victims are more likely to accept the request or click on any links sent in subsequent messages.

Once the victim clicks on a malicious link, they may be directed to a phishing website or asked to download harmful software. Scammers can then collect login credentials, personal information, or even install malware on the victim's device, potentially leading to more significant security breaches.

5. Verification Scams

Verification scams target users, especially those with large followings, by offering them the opportunity to become "verified" on a social media platform. The scam usually starts with a message claiming to be from the platform's support team, stating that the user qualifies for account verification or that their account is under review for suspicious activity. The user is then asked to click on a link and enter their login credentials to verify their identity.

In reality, the link leads to a phishing page where scammers steal the user's login information. Once they have access to the account, they may lock the user out and use the account for other fraudulent activities.

The Impact of Phishing Scams on Victims

Phishing scams can have devastating consequences for victims. In many cases, stolen login credentials allow scammers to take control of social media accounts, locking users out of their profiles and causing significant reputational damage. Once in control, scammers may use the hacked account to send more phishing messages, spread malware, or scam the victim's friends and family.

Beyond the immediate loss of access to social media accounts, phishing victims often face financial harm. Scammers may use stolen credit card information to make unauthorized purchases or use personal details for identity theft. The emotional toll on victims can also be considerable, as they grapple with the violation of their privacy and the potential damage to their personal and professional lives.

How to Protect Yourself from Phishing Scams on Social Media

Despite the sophisticated tactics employed by scammers, there are several ways you can protect yourself from falling victim to phishing scams on social media.

1. Be Cautious of Unsolicited Messages

If you receive an unsolicited message from someone you don't know or a suspicious message from a friend, proceed with caution. Even if the message appears to come from someone you trust, their account could have been hacked. Avoid clicking on any links or downloading attachments without verifying the message's legitimacy through a separate communication channel.

2. Verify the Source of Links

Before clicking on any link, especially if it was sent via social media, hover over the link to preview the URL. If the URL looks suspicious or does not match the expected destination, do not click on it. Scammers often use URLs that closely resemble legitimate websites but with minor changes in spelling or domain extensions to trick users.

3. Use Two-Factor Authentication

Enabling two-factor authentication (2FA) on your social media accounts adds an extra layer of security. Even if a scammer manages to steal your login credentials, they will still need access to your secondary authentication method, such as a code sent to your phone, to log in.

4. Keep Software Updated

Make sure your devices and social media apps are running the latest security updates. Scammers often exploit vulnerabilities in outdated software to launch attacks, so keeping your devices updated can help protect you from known threats.

5. Report Suspicious Activity

If you encounter a phishing scam or notice unusual activity on your account, report it to the social media platform immediately. Platforms like Facebook and Twitter (X) have mechanisms in place for reporting phishing attempts and suspicious profiles. By reporting these scams, you can help prevent others from falling victim.

Conclusion

Phishing scams on social media represent a serious and evolving threat in the digital age. Cybercriminals use social engineering tactics to exploit users' trust, leading them to click on malicious links or provide sensitive information. As these scams become more sophisticated, it is essential to stay vigilant and take proactive steps to protect your personal information online. By understanding how phishing scams work and being cautious about the messages and links you interact with on social media, you can significantly reduce your risk of becoming a victim of these fraudulent schemes.

Chapter 7. Romance Scams
Love in the Time of Fraud

Introduction

In an era where digital communication has reshaped the landscape of relationships, many have found solace in the connectivity offered by social media platforms and online dating sites. However, with this unprecedented convenience also comes a dark side - romance scams. These scams target vulnerable individuals, preying on emotions, trust, and the human desire for companionship. As online dating continues to grow, so do the dangers associated with fraudulent schemes masquerading as love stories. This chapter delves into the world of romance scams, shedding light on how these deceitful plots operate and why they are so effective in today's digitally connected world.

The Rise of Online Romance

The advent of the internet has transformed the way people meet and form relationships. Online dating platforms, such as Tinder, Bumble, and Match, alongside social media platforms like Facebook and Instagram, provide a space for individuals to forge connections that might have been impossible in traditional face-to-face settings. These platforms eliminate geographical barriers and allow people to communicate with potential partners across the globe.

Yet, the anonymity that online communication affords also makes it easier for scammers to create false personas and narratives. Scammers can quickly craft an attractive online presence, complete with photos, backstories, and carefully curated details that appeal to their targets. Once trust is established, they begin the manipulation process. These scammers often invest significant time and effort in building a relationship, waiting for the right moment to take advantage of their victim's trust and emotions.

How Romance Scams Work

Romance scams typically follow a predictable pattern, although the specifics can vary from one case to another. It begins with the scammer contacting the victim, usually on an online dating site or social media platform. The scammer creates a profile that appears legitimate - complete with photos, interests, and a compelling backstory. These profiles are often tailored to appeal to the victim's preferences or vulnerabilities.

In many cases, the scammer portrays themselves as an attractive, successful individual looking for love. They might claim to be a businessperson, military officer, or humanitarian working in a foreign country - positions that help explain their inability to meet in person while also generating sympathy. The scammer will communicate with the victim regularly, often showering them with attention and affection, and building a strong emotional bond.

Once the victim's trust is secured, the scammer begins to manipulate them into sending money, often for fabricated emergencies such as medical bills, travel expenses, or legal troubles. In some cases, scammers will maintain the ruse for months or even years, continuing to drain the victim's finances until the victim either runs out of money or grows suspicious.

The Emotional Manipulation Behind Romance Scams

What makes romance scams so effective is the emotional manipulation involved. Scammers know how to exploit human vulnerability, particularly the longing for love and companionship. Many victims of romance scams are people who feel isolated, lonely, or unloved, making them more susceptible to emotional deception.

The scammer invests time in learning about their victim's life, hopes, and dreams. By doing so, they create a seemingly genuine connection that makes the victim feel special and loved. Over time, the victim becomes emotionally dependent on the scammer, making it difficult for them to recognize the red flags. This emotional investment can cloud their judgment, leading them to trust the scammer implicitly and take irrational actions, such as sending large sums of money or sharing personal information.

The Financial Impact of Romance Scams

While romance scams are emotionally devastating, their financial toll can be equally crippling. Victims of these scams often lose thousands - or even hundreds of thousands - of dollars to their online "lovers." In some cases, victims take out loans, empty their savings accounts, or sell valuable assets to provide financial support to their scammer. Once the scam is uncovered, victims are left not only heartbroken but also financially ruined.

According to the Federal Trade Commission (FTC), romance scams are among the most financially damaging forms of online fraud. In 2020 alone, victims in the U.S. reported losing over $304 million to romance scams. The global reach of these scams means that people from all walks of life, regardless of their age, gender, or location, are vulnerable.

In addition to financial loss, many victims experience long-term emotional and psychological consequences. The realization that they have been scammed by someone they trusted can lead to feelings of shame, guilt, and self-blame. Some victims may struggle to trust others in future relationships, both online and offline.

Red Flags and Warning Signs

Romance scams can be difficult to detect, especially when the scammer is highly skilled in manipulation. However, there are several red flags that can help individuals recognize when they might be dealing with a romance scammer.

1. Requests for Money: **A common characteristic of romance scams is the scammer eventually asking the victim for money. They may concoct stories about medical emergencies, stranded travel situations, or legal troubles and plead for financial assistance.**

2. Avoidance of In-Person Meetings: **Scammers often make excuses to avoid meeting their victim in person. They may claim to be working in a remote or dangerous location or pretend they are unable to travel due to logistical or financial issues.**

3. Inconsistencies in Their Story: **Scammers may slip up and provide inconsistent details about their background or situation. They might change details about where they live, their job, or their family over time.**

4. Too Good to Be True: **If someone online seems too perfect - unbelievably attractive, wealthy, and emotionally available - it may be a sign of a scam. Scammers create idealized personas to lure victims into their trap.**

5. **Pressure to Move the Relationship Forward Quickly:** Scammers often push to escalate the relationship quickly, proclaiming love or deep emotional connections after only a short time. This is done to create a sense of urgency and prevent the victim from questioning the relationship.

The Role of Social Media in Facilitating Scams

Social media has become a fertile ground for romance scammers, largely due to the ease with which fake accounts can be created and maintained. Platforms like Facebook, Instagram, and even LinkedIn provide scammers with access to a wealth of personal information about their potential targets, which can be used to craft convincing personas.

Moreover, the anonymity of social media allows scammers to avoid detection and consequences. Many romance scammers operate from foreign countries, making it difficult for law enforcement agencies to track them down and hold them accountable. Social media platforms have tried to crack down on fake profiles and online fraud, but the sheer volume of accounts makes it challenging to catch every scammer.

Despite these efforts, social media platforms remain popular hunting grounds for romance scammers. The sense of legitimacy that comes with having a social media profile makes it easier for scammers to build trust with their victims, and many people let their guard down when interacting with someone they believe to be authentic.

Why People Fall for Romance Scams

Romance scams prey on deep-seated emotional needs, and it's important to understand why people fall for these schemes despite the obvious risks. Several psychological and situational factors contribute to a person's vulnerability to romance scams.

1. Loneliness: Many victims of romance scams are lonely, either because they live alone or because they feel disconnected from their social circles. This loneliness makes them more likely to seek out companionship online, where they are at risk of encountering scammers.

2. Trust in Online Relationships: The rise of online dating has normalized the idea of forming deep emotional connections with people we've never met in person. For many, the distinction between online and offline relationships has blurred, making it easier for scammers to exploit these connections.

3. The Halo Effect: Scammers often present themselves as highly attractive and successful individuals, which can cause victims to overlook red flags. This phenomenon, known as the "halo effect," leads people to assume that someone who looks good and says the right things must also have good intentions.

4. Cognitive Dissonance: Once a victim has invested time and emotion into an online relationship, it becomes difficult for them to accept that they've been scammed. This cognitive dissonance can lead them to rationalize away suspicious behavior and continue to trust the scammer despite mounting evidence.

Protecting Yourself from Romance Scams

The best defense against romance scams is awareness. By understanding how these scams work and recognizing the red flags, individuals can protect themselves from becoming victims. Here are a few tips to stay safe.

Verify their Identity: Before getting emotionally involved with someone you meet online, take the time to verify their identity. Perform a reverse image search on their profile pictures to see if they've been used elsewhere, and look for inconsistencies in their story.

Never Send Money: If someone you've met online asks for money, it's almost always a scam. No matter how convincing their story may be, it's important to remember that legitimate romantic partners don't ask for financial assistance from people they've never met in person.

Keep Personal Information Private: Don't share sensitive personal information, such as your home address, financial details, or passwords, with someone you've only interacted with online.

Report Suspicious Behavior: If you suspect that you're being targeted by a romance scammer, report their profile to the platform you're using. Many social media and dating sites have mechanisms in place to remove fake accounts and prevent fraud.

Conclusion

Romance scams represent a heartbreaking intersection of trust, vulnerability, and deception in the digital age. While technology has expanded the ways in which we can connect with others, it has also opened the door for scammers to exploit those seeking companionship. The emotional and financial toll of these scams can be devastating, but by staying informed and vigilant, individuals can protect themselves and others from falling victim to fraud in the guise of love.

Chapter 8. Catfishing
Behind the Mask

Introduction

In the ever-evolving world of social media and online interactions, our identities have become fluid. We are no longer limited to the constraints of geography, and the anonymity offered by the internet allows us to connect with people from different cultures, backgrounds, and walks of life. But with this expanded world of opportunities comes the dark side of human interaction: the rise of online scams. Among the most prevalent and psychologically damaging of these is catfishing, a term that refers to the practice of using a fabricated online persona to deceive and manipulate individuals. This article delves deep into the mechanics of catfishing, exploring how scammers fabricate entire identities, the psychology behind why victims fall prey, and the emotional and financial toll it takes on those targeted.

What Is Catfishing?

Catfishing is the act of creating a false identity online, typically for the purpose of deceiving someone else into a romantic or emotional relationship. In this digital age, where meeting and interacting with people online has become normalized, scammers exploit this medium by constructing fictitious personas. These fraudulent identities are often meticulously crafted to appear authentic, from the use of fake photos and stolen bios to fabricated personal histories. Catfishers hide behind these fake masks, gaining the trust of their victims over time, sometimes for weeks, months, or even years.

At its core, catfishing relies on the emotional manipulation of individuals who are seeking companionship, love, or understanding in the vast online world. While some instances of catfishing are simply carried out for emotional satisfaction, many perpetrators engage in this deceit for financial gain. Romance scams have become increasingly common, with criminals using the guise of a loving relationship to extort money from their victims.

The Mechanics of Catfishing

One might wonder how an individual could fall for a fabricated persona. After all, wouldn't inconsistencies or lack of in-person interaction raise red flags? Unfortunately, catfishers have developed sophisticated methods to avoid detection and perpetuate the deception.

First, the anonymity provided by the internet allows the scammer to avoid real-life encounters, offering plausible excuses for why they can't meet in person. These excuses may range from financial difficulties to geographic distance or even health issues. Additionally, catfishers often use photos of attractive or charismatic individuals to enhance their appeal, pulling their victims into a web of fantasy. Social media accounts, email addresses, and even phone numbers are often linked to these fake personas, adding layers of perceived authenticity.

Scammers also play the long game. Building an emotional connection over weeks or months can establish trust and affection, making the victim less suspicious and more inclined to believe the authenticity of the relationship. This emotional manipulation is at the heart of the catfishing scheme: the scammer preys on the victim's vulnerabilities, crafting a narrative that aligns with their desires and emotional needs.

Psychological Tactics of Catfishers

The success of catfishing lies in the ability of scammers to psychologically manipulate their victims. One of the key strategies they use is love-bombing - an intense and often overwhelming display of affection in the early stages of the relationship. The scammer may send frequent messages of admiration, declare love early on, and make grand promises of a future together. This barrage of affection serves to rapidly create emotional intimacy, making the victim feel special and valued.

Another common tactic is the damsel in distress narrative. The scammer may create a storyline in which they are facing dire circumstances - such as an urgent financial crisis or personal tragedy. These fabricated hardships often lead to the scammer asking for money, with the victim feeling compelled to help someone they believe they care about deeply. The scammer exploits their victim's empathy and sense of responsibility, ensuring that the victim feels they are supporting a loved one in need.

Finally, gaslighting - a form of psychological manipulation where the scammer makes the victim question their own judgment - often plays a role in these scams. If the victim begins to express doubt or suspicion, the scammer may twist the narrative, accuse the victim of mistrust, or create false evidence to back up their claims. This manipulation can erode the victim's self-confidence and make them more susceptible to further deceit.

The Financial Side of Catfishing

Although some catfishers engage in this practice for emotional satisfaction, many have a more tangible motive:

financial gain. According to the Federal Trade Commission, romance scams have become one of the most financially devastating forms of online fraud, with millions of dollars being siphoned from victims each year.

Scammers often ask for money under the guise of an emergency. For example, the scammer may claim to be stuck in a foreign country and need funds for a flight home, or they may pretend to have a medical condition requiring urgent treatment. Because the emotional bond has already been established, the victim may feel an obligation to help, believing that they are aiding a partner in need. Once the money is sent, the requests often escalate, with the scammer concocting additional emergencies or difficulties.

In more advanced cases, some catfishers involve their victims in money-laundering schemes without their knowledge. The victim may be asked to send or receive funds on behalf of the scammer, unaware that they are being used as a conduit for illicit transactions. This can have severe legal consequences for the victim, who may be implicated in financial crimes despite having no knowledge of their involvement.

The Emotional and Psychological Toll on Victims

The emotional devastation caused by catfishing can be profound. Victims often describe feeling a deep sense of betrayal, as they believed they were in a genuine, loving relationship, only to discover that the person they cared for never truly existed. The realization that their emotions were manipulated for personal gain can lead to long-lasting psychological damage, including depression, anxiety, and trust issues.

The embarrassment and shame of falling for a scam also prevent many victims from seeking help or reporting the incident. They may fear being judged for their naivety or for trusting someone they never met in person. This can lead to isolation, as the victim withdraws from social circles and becomes wary of future relationships.

The financial loss, too, can be overwhelming, particularly for those who have sent significant amounts of money to the scammer. Many victims find themselves in financial ruin, having drained their savings or even taken out loans to support the scammer's fictitious needs. The combination of emotional and financial devastation can be crippling, leaving victims struggling to recover both psychologically and materially.

Why Do People Fall for Catfishing?

To outsiders, it may seem unfathomable that someone could fall for a relationship based entirely on digital interaction, but the reasons victims are vulnerable to catfishing are complex and deeply rooted in human psychology.

Many victims are lonely, seeking companionship or emotional connection in a world where online interaction has become the norm. The internet provides a space where individuals can present the best version of themselves, often allowing for a level of vulnerability and openness that might not exist in face-to-face relationships. Catfishers exploit this vulnerability, offering a sense of emotional safety and acceptance that is deeply attractive to those seeking love or companionship.

In other cases, victims may be going through a difficult time in their lives, such as a recent breakup, job loss, or other emotional challenges. The scammer's attention, affection, and apparent interest in the victim's well-being can be a lifeline during these difficult periods. When someone is emotionally vulnerable, they are more likely to overlook red flags and place their trust in someone who appears to offer comfort and support.

Warning Signs of a Catfish

While catfishers are skilled at deception, there are often warning signs that can indicate something is amiss. A reluctance to meet in person or have a video chat is one of the most common red flags. The scammer may provide excuses such as being too busy, living too far away, or facing personal issues that prevent them from meeting.

Additionally, a catfisher may have inconsistencies in their story or personal details. They may claim to have a high-profile job or a glamorous lifestyle, yet their social media presence doesn't align with these claims. Victims should also be wary of individuals who ask for money early in the relationship, particularly for vague or urgent reasons.

If someone seems too perfect or the relationship progresses too quickly, it may be a sign that the individual is not who they claim to be. Trusting instincts and paying attention to inconsistencies can help prevent falling victim to these scams.

Conclusion: The Path to Awareness

Catfishing, at its core, is an act of deception that preys on the emotional vulnerabilities of its victims. It is a reminder of the dangers that lurk behind the screens of our devices, where trust can be easily manipulated by those with malicious intent. The emotional and financial toll of catfishing is severe, leaving victims devastated and struggling to rebuild their lives.

However, with greater awareness of the warning signs and a deeper understanding of the psychological tactics used by catfishers, individuals can protect themselves from falling victim to these scams. The path to awareness begins with education - understanding that not everything we see online is what it appears to be. By fostering a culture of caution and open dialogue about online relationships, we can begin to dismantle the mask of catfishing and prevent future scams.

Chapter 9. Fraud through Impersonation
From CEOs to Commoners

Introduction

In today's hyper-connected digital world, fraud through impersonation has emerged as one of the most prevalent and damaging forms of online scams. From high-profile individuals such as CEOs and public figures to everyday users of social media, no one is immune to the deceptive tactics employed by fraudsters. These scams not only damage reputations but also have devastating financial consequences for victims. As impersonation fraud continues to rise, understanding how it occurs, its implications, and ways to protect oneself is crucial.

The Rise of Impersonation Fraud

Impersonation fraud is not a new phenomenon, but the digital age has provided an ideal environment for scammers to thrive. In the past, impersonation was limited to physical interactions, such as someone pretending to be a company employee or official. However, with the advent of social media and other online platforms, fraudsters can now impersonate individuals on a much larger scale, often without the need for physical presence.

This form of fraud occurs when a scammer pretends to be someone else, usually a trusted person or an authority figure, to deceive and manipulate others into providing sensitive information, transferring money, or granting access to personal accounts. These impersonations can target anyone from CEOs of major corporations to everyday users of social media platforms, making it a universal threat.

The primary appeal of impersonation fraud lies in the fact that trust is often implicit in relationships, especially in professional settings. When someone receives an email from their CEO or a direct message from a friend on social media, they are less likely to question the authenticity of the communication. Fraudsters exploit this trust, using social engineering tactics to trick victims into compliance.

Impersonating High-Profile Individuals: The CEO Fraud

One of the most alarming forms of impersonation fraud is the "CEO fraud", also known as Business Email Compromise (BEC). This scam typically targets companies by impersonating a high-ranking executive, such as a CEO or CFO, to trick employees into transferring funds to the fraudster's account. This type of fraud is particularly devastating because of the significant amounts of money that can be involved.

In a typical CEO fraud scheme, the scammer gains access to or creates a fake email account that closely resembles the CEO's actual address. Using this fake identity, the fraudster sends urgent emails to lower-level employees, typically in finance or accounting, instructing them to wire large sums of money to a seemingly legitimate business partner or vendor. The employee, believing they are acting on direct orders from their superior, complies without questioning the request. By the time the scam is discovered, the money is often long gone, having been funneled through multiple accounts to obscure its trail.

The financial impact of CEO fraud can be enormous. According to the FBI, BEC scams have cost businesses over $26 billion globally from 2016 to 2020, with losses steadily increasing each year. Large corporations are often the primary targets because of their significant financial resources, but smaller companies are not immune. In many cases, these smaller businesses lack the internal controls necessary to detect such scams, making them particularly vulnerable.

Aside from the financial losses, CEO fraud can also damage a company's reputation and relationships with its clients and vendors. If a business partner discovers that they were unknowingly involved in a fraudulent transaction, it can erode trust and lead to legal repercussions. Furthermore, the internal fallout from such an incident can damage employee morale and shake confidence in leadership.

Social Media Impersonation: Targeting the Common User

While high-profile individuals and businesses are prime targets for impersonation fraud, ordinary social media users are not spared. In fact, fraudsters frequently impersonate common users to carry out scams, often exploiting the casual, personal nature of these platforms to deceive their victims. This type of impersonation fraud can take various forms, from cloning a user's profile to creating entirely fictitious accounts that resemble real people.

One common tactic is "profile cloning", in which a fraudster creates a duplicate of an existing user's social media profile. The scammer then sends friend requests to the victim's friends and family, posing as the victim. Once trust is established, the fraudster proceeds to ask for money, claiming to be in an emergency, such as a lost wallet, medical expenses, or other urgent needs. Friends and family, believing they are helping someone they know, may comply with the requests, only to later discover that they have been duped.

Another method involves creating fake accounts that appear to represent legitimate businesses or government agencies. These accounts are used to target common users with phishing schemes, where victims are tricked into providing personal information, such as credit card numbers, bank details, or social security numbers. In many cases, these scams are highly sophisticated, with the fake profiles mirroring official pages down to the smallest details, making it difficult for users to distinguish them from the real thing.

The financial impact of social media impersonation fraud is often less than that of CEO fraud but can still be devastating for the victims. For many individuals, the sums of money lost in these scams represent significant portions of their savings or emergency funds. Additionally, the emotional toll of being deceived by someone they believed to be a trusted friend or loved one can be substantial.

The Mechanics of Impersonation: How Scammers Execute Their Schemes

To understand how fraudsters are so successful in impersonation scams, it is essential to examine the mechanics behind their schemes. These scams often rely on social engineering techniques, which manipulate human emotions and behaviors to achieve the desired outcome.

Fraudsters begin by gathering information about their targets. In the case of CEO fraud, this might involve researching a company's hierarchy, identifying key decision-makers, and learning about ongoing business transactions or relationships with vendors. This information allows the scammer to craft convincing emails or messages that appear legitimate.

In social media impersonation fraud, scammers often study the profiles of their targets, looking for clues about their personal lives, relationships, and communication styles. This helps them replicate the victim's online presence more convincingly and make their messages seem authentic. Once they have gained access to the victim's social network, they use social engineering tactics to prey on their emotions, such as urgency, fear, or guilt, to elicit the desired response.

The use of technology also plays a significant role in these scams. Fraudsters can easily create fake email addresses, duplicate social media profiles, and even manipulate phone numbers to make their impersonation more credible. In some cases, they use more advanced techniques, such as deepfake technology, to create realistic audio or video recordings of the person they are impersonating.

The Financial Impact of Impersonation Fraud

The financial implications of impersonation fraud are severe, both for individuals and businesses. For corporations, CEO fraud can result in millions of dollars in losses, as well as additional costs related to legal fees, investigations, and implementing stricter security protocols. Small businesses may be forced to close their doors if they fall victim to such scams, unable to recover from the financial blow.

For individual victims of social media impersonation fraud, the losses may not be as large, but they are often just as devastating. Victims may lose their savings, incur debt, or have their credit ruined as a result of these scams. In some cases, the financial loss is compounded by the emotional toll of being deceived by someone they trusted.

Moreover, impersonation fraud can have a ripple effect on the broader economy. When businesses lose significant sums of money to fraud, they may be forced to lay off employees, reduce investment in innovation, or pass on the costs to consumers in the form of higher prices. On a larger scale, widespread fraud undermines trust in digital platforms, making individuals and businesses more hesitant to engage in online transactions, which can stifle economic growth.

Combating Impersonation Fraud: Prevention and Protection

Preventing impersonation fraud requires a combination of technological solutions, employee training, and public awareness. For businesses, implementing stricter security protocols, such as two-factor authentication, email verification, and regular security audits, can help reduce the risk of CEO fraud. Employees should be trained to recognize the warning signs of phishing emails and to verify any suspicious requests for money or sensitive information.

On social media, users can protect themselves by adjusting their privacy settings to limit the amount of personal information visible to the public. They should also be cautious about accepting friend requests from unfamiliar accounts, even if they appear to be from someone they know. Additionally, reporting suspicious activity to the platform can help prevent further scams.

Public awareness campaigns can also play a vital role in reducing impersonation fraud. By educating people about the dangers of these scams and how to recognize them, governments, businesses, and social media platforms can empower individuals to protect themselves.

Conclusion

Fraud through impersonation, whether targeting high-profile CEOs or common social media users, is a growing threat in the digital age. The financial and emotional impact on victims can be devastating, with losses ranging from a few hundred dollars to millions. As fraudsters continue to evolve their tactics, it is essential for businesses and individuals to remain vigilant and take proactive steps to protect themselves from this insidious form of online fraud. By understanding the mechanics of impersonation scams and implementing preventive measures, we can reduce the risk and protect ourselves from falling victim to these deceitful schemes.

Chapter 10. Influencer Fraud
Fake Followers and Endorsements

Introduction

In recent years, influencer marketing has emerged as a powerful tool for brands to connect with their audiences. Platforms like Instagram, YouTube, and TikTok have transformed ordinary individuals into internet celebrities, wielding considerable influence over consumer behavior. The appeal of influencers lies in their perceived authenticity and their ability to engage audiences on a more personal level than traditional advertising. However, alongside the growth of this industry, a darker side has emerged - one marked by fraud, fake followers, and deceptive endorsements. Influencer fraud has become a significant issue, not only undermining the trust of followers but also costing brands millions in wasted marketing dollars.

The Rise of Influencers and Their Economic Impact

The global influencer marketing industry is projected to surpass $21 billion by 2024. Brands are willing to pay influencers substantial sums to promote their products, with some top-tier influencers earning as much as $1 million per post. Micro-influencers, who typically have fewer followers, can still command respectable fees, with brands willing to invest due to the influencers' perceived engagement and authenticity. However, as money poured into this growing ecosystem, so too did opportunities for manipulation and fraud. The financial rewards of being a successful influencer have motivated some to artificially inflate their follower counts and engagement metrics, often at the expense of both their audience's trust and the brands they collaborate with.

What Is Influencer Fraud?

Influencer fraud occurs when influencers or individuals representing them use dishonest tactics to appear more influential than they really are. This type of fraud can take various forms, but the most common include purchasing fake followers, artificially inflating engagement metrics like likes and comments, and faking endorsements to gain the trust of followers and brand deals. The prevalence of these practices has made it difficult for brands to distinguish between genuine influencers and those who manipulate their statistics for personal or financial gain.

At its core, influencer fraud is about deception - manipulating numbers and projecting a false image of influence. This deception can have widespread consequences, damaging the credibility of the influencer marketing industry as a whole. As trust diminishes, brands may become hesitant to invest in influencer campaigns, fearing that their partnerships may not deliver the promised return on investment.

Fake Followers: The Core of the Problem

One of the most common forms of influencer fraud involves purchasing fake followers. A significant portion of the influencer ecosystem revolves around the size of one's following. The larger the audience, the higher the likelihood that a brand will see the influencer as a valuable marketing partner. This has led some influencers, particularly those trying to break into the industry, to artificially inflate their follower count by purchasing followers from third-party services.

Fake followers are typically bots - automated accounts that are programmed to follow certain users. While they may boost an influencer's follower count, they do not engage with content in a meaningful way. This lack of real engagement can lead to skewed metrics, making it difficult for brands to accurately measure the success of their influencer campaigns.

The consequences of fake followers extend beyond wasted marketing dollars. When influencers deceive brands by inflating their follower counts, they are undermining the trust that forms the foundation of the influencer-brand relationship. Brands invest in influencer partnerships based on the assumption that the influencer can effectively reach a target audience. When that audience turns out to be largely composed of bots, the entire marketing campaign becomes ineffective, leading to a loss of trust between the influencer and the brand.

Fake Engagement: Inflating Likes, Comments, and Views

Beyond follower counts, engagement metrics like likes, comments, and views are also critical indicators of an influencer's reach and influence. Brands are often more interested in how engaged an influencer's audience is, rather than just the size of their following. However, influencers can also manipulate these metrics to make it appear as though they have higher engagement rates than they truly do.

Fake engagement typically involves the use of engagement pods, where influencers agree to like, comment on, or share each other's posts to boost their visibility. While this practice may not seem as deceitful as purchasing fake followers, it still creates a false impression of how popular or influential an individual is. In some cases, influencers may also buy fake likes, comments, or views from third-party services. This is particularly common on platforms like Instagram, where visual engagement is key to determining the success of a post.

In an industry that thrives on authenticity, fake engagement undermines the very qualities that make influencer marketing effective. Brands are seeking to connect with genuine communities through their partnerships with influencers. However, when influencers artificially boost their engagement rates, they are creating a facade of popularity, leading brands to believe that their campaigns are more successful than they truly are.

Fake Endorsements: Misleading Consumers

Influencer fraud extends beyond fake followers and engagement metrics. Another form of deception that has become increasingly common involves fake endorsements. In this scenario, influencers may promote products or services they have not actually used or endorse brands that have not officially partnered with them. This practice is especially harmful to consumers, who trust influencers' recommendations based on the assumption that they are genuine.

Fake endorsements can take several forms. Some influencers may accept money from brands without disclosing their relationship, which violates regulations set by governing bodies like the Federal Trade Commission (FTC). In other cases, influencers may claim to be affiliated with a brand in order to appear more credible, when in reality, no such partnership exists. The result is a lack of transparency, leading consumers to make purchasing decisions based on false information.

This type of deception not only damages the trust between influencers and their followers but also jeopardizes the credibility of influencer marketing as a whole. When consumers realize that they have been misled by influencers they once trusted, they may become more skeptical of future endorsements, making it harder for genuine influencers to maintain their credibility.

Financial Gain at the Expense of Authenticity

The financial incentives for influencer fraud are clear. With brands paying top dollar for influencer partnerships, there is a strong motivation for individuals to inflate their influence in order to secure lucrative deals. Unfortunately, this has led to a growing number of influencers prioritizing short-term financial gain over long-term authenticity and credibility.

For many influencers, the desire to maintain a certain lifestyle - one that is often portrayed as glamorous and financially rewarding - fuels the temptation to engage in fraudulent practices. Influencers may feel pressure to present a certain image to their followers and sponsors, even if it means resorting to dishonest tactics to uphold that image. As a result, many influencers are willing to cut corners and engage in fraudulent activities in order to sustain their brand.

The consequences of this behavior are far-reaching. Not only do brands waste money on ineffective campaigns, but followers also lose trust in the influencers they once admired. In the long run, influencer fraud erodes the very foundation of the influencer marketing industry, making it harder for genuine influencers to succeed without resorting to dishonest tactics.

The Impact on Brands and Consumers

Influencer fraud is not just a problem for influencers - it has serious consequences for brands and consumers as well. For brands, the financial cost of working with fraudulent influencers can be significant. In 2019 alone, influencer fraud cost brands an estimated $1.3 billion in wasted marketing dollars. This is money that could have been better spent on genuine influencer partnerships or other marketing strategies.

For consumers, the impact of influencer fraud is more personal. Many people follow influencers because they believe in their authenticity and trust their recommendations. When influencers deceive their audience by using fake followers or endorsing products they have not actually used, it damages the trust that consumers have in both the influencer and the brands they promote.

Moreover, the widespread nature of influencer fraud can create a general sense of skepticism among consumers, making it harder for legitimate influencers to build and maintain their credibility. As trust erodes, consumers may become less likely to engage with influencer content, which in turn reduces the effectiveness of influencer marketing as a whole.

Combating Influencer Fraud: A Collaborative Effort

The fight against influencer fraud requires a collaborative effort from both brands and social media platforms. Brands can take steps to protect themselves from fraudulent influencers by conducting thorough vetting processes before entering into partnerships. This includes analyzing engagement metrics to ensure that an influencer's audience is genuine and actively engaged.

Social media platforms also play a critical role in combating influencer fraud. Many platforms have implemented measures to detect and remove fake accounts, as well as tools to help brands identify fraudulent influencers. For example, Instagram has cracked down on the purchase of fake followers and likes, while YouTube has introduced stricter guidelines for content creators.

Despite these efforts, influencer fraud remains a persistent issue. As long as there are financial incentives for influencers to inflate their statistics, there will always be individuals willing to engage in dishonest practices. However, by working together, brands, platforms, and consumers can help to reduce the prevalence of influencer fraud and create a more transparent and trustworthy influencer marketing industry.

Conclusion

Influencer fraud poses a significant threat to the integrity of the influencer marketing industry. By using fake followers, engagement, and endorsements, influencers deceive brands and consumers alike for financial gain. This deception not only costs brands millions in wasted marketing dollars but also erodes the trust that is essential to the success of influencer marketing. While efforts to combat influencer fraud are underway, it remains a persistent problem that requires ongoing vigilance from brands, social media platforms, and consumers. Only through collaboration and transparency can the industry move toward a future where authenticity and trust are at the forefront of influencer marketing.

Chapter 11. AI-Driven Scams
Synthetic Voices and Real Threats

Introduction

In today's digital age, artificial intelligence (AI) has opened doors to both innovative solutions and unprecedented risks. While AI-driven tools have enhanced sectors like healthcare, finance, and entertainment, they have also provided malicious actors with the means to conduct increasingly sophisticated scams. Among the most concerning developments in the realm of AI fraud are synthetic voices, which allow scammers to convincingly mimic trusted individuals. This growing threat represents a real and urgent danger, with profound implications for victims who may find it difficult, if not impossible, to differentiate between real and fake communications.

The Rise of AI-Generated Voices

Synthetic voices, often referred to as "deepfake" audio, are created through advanced AI techniques such as machine learning and neural networks. These technologies can analyze vast amounts of data from a person's voice recordings and generate speech that is nearly indistinguishable from the original speaker. This ability to clone a voice has been rapidly evolving, with AI systems now capable of generating synthetic voices from just a few seconds of audio input.

The technology is widely accessible and can be used for legitimate purposes, such as enabling voice assistants, enhancing entertainment through synthesized celebrity voices, or allowing individuals with speech impairments to communicate using customized voice models. However, in the wrong hands, these capabilities are being exploited to create highly convincing scams.

How AI-Generated Voice Scams Work

AI-driven scams using synthetic voices generally follow a pattern designed to exploit the victim's trust. By mimicking the voice of someone the victim knows - such as a family member, friend, or even a business executive - scammers can manipulate targets into performing actions that they would not normally do, such as transferring money, providing sensitive information, or granting access to secure systems.

One common example involves what is often referred to as the "CEO scam." In these scenarios, an employee receives a phone call from someone who appears to be a senior executive within the company. The caller, using a synthetic voice generated from recordings of the executive, requests an urgent wire transfer or the sharing of confidential information. Because the voice sounds genuine, the employee complies, leading to financial losses or data breaches.

In other cases, scammers may pose as a loved one in distress. A victim may receive a call from someone who sounds exactly like their child, spouse, or close friend, claiming that they are in immediate danger and need money or assistance. These emotionally charged scenarios are designed to bypass rational thinking, pushing victims to act quickly without questioning the authenticity of the call.

The Psychological Impact on Victims

The success of AI-generated voice scams is rooted not just in the technology's ability to replicate human voices but in its exploitation of trust and emotion. When a person hears a familiar voice asking for help or making an urgent request, they are less likely to doubt the authenticity of the communication. This is particularly true in situations where the scammer capitalizes on the victim's emotional vulnerability, such as by pretending to be a loved one in trouble.

For victims, the psychological impact of these scams can be devastating. Beyond the immediate financial loss or compromise of personal information, there is often a profound sense of betrayal and fear. The realization that the voice they trusted was an imposter can lead to feelings of violation and confusion, as well as long-term anxiety about whether they will be able to trust future communications from people they care about.

Additionally, the sense of helplessness that accompanies these scams is amplified by the fact that, for many, the technology involved is difficult to comprehend. Victims may struggle to understand how their loved one's voice was cloned or why they failed to recognize the scam, further compounding their distress.

The Threat to Businesses and Organizations

AI-driven voice scams are not limited to individual victims. Businesses and organizations are also at significant risk. In the corporate world, executives' voices are often publicly available through speeches, interviews, and conference calls. Scammers can easily harvest this data to generate synthetic voices, enabling them to carry out attacks such as the aforementioned CEO scams or to orchestrate large-scale fraud.

One notable example occurred in 2019, when a UK-based energy firm was defrauded of $243,000. The company's CEO received a call from what sounded like the voice of the CEO of its parent company, instructing him to make an urgent payment to a Hungarian supplier. The CEO, trusting the voice, complied, only to later discover that the call had been generated using AI. Cases like this highlight the growing risk of voice fraud to businesses and the potentially massive financial consequences.

The rise of AI-generated voice scams has also prompted concerns about cybersecurity. Traditional security measures, such as two-factor authentication, may not be sufficient to protect against these attacks, as they rely on the assumption that only authorized individuals can make certain requests. When scammers can convincingly impersonate those individuals, even the most vigilant employees may be deceived.

Implications for Law Enforcement and Cybersecurity

The emergence of synthetic voice scams presents significant challenges for law enforcement and cybersecurity professionals. Investigating these crimes is inherently difficult because the use of AI enables scammers to operate from anywhere in the world while masking their true identity. Moreover, the technology used to create synthetic voices is constantly improving, making it harder to detect fraudulent calls or verify the authenticity of voice communications.

Traditional methods of combatting fraud, such as recognizing suspicious phone numbers or email addresses, may not be as effective when it comes to AI-generated scams. Since the scammer's voice sounds identical to a trusted individual, even sophisticated detection systems may struggle to flag these communications as fraudulent.

To address this challenge, cybersecurity experts are developing new techniques to detect AI-generated audio. For example, researchers are working on algorithms that can analyze subtle inconsistencies in synthetic speech, such as unnatural pauses, cadence, or background noise that does not match the environment. However, these systems are still in development and may not be widely available for some time.

Law enforcement agencies are also grappling with the question of how to prosecute individuals involved in AI-driven scams. Many countries' legal frameworks have not yet caught up to the technological advancements in this area, making it difficult to hold perpetrators accountable. Furthermore, the international nature of many AI-driven scams complicates efforts to bring scammers to justice, as they often operate across borders, using anonymizing tools to evade detection.

The Role of Public Awareness and Education

As AI-generated voice scams continue to proliferate, public awareness and education will be critical in mitigating their impact. Many victims are not aware of the existence of synthetic voices or the potential for AI to be used in scams, leaving them vulnerable to exploitation.

Educational campaigns should focus on informing individuals and businesses about the risks of AI-generated voice fraud and offering practical advice on how to protect themselves. For instance, individuals can be encouraged to verify any unexpected requests for money or sensitive information through alternative means, such as calling the person directly on a known phone number or using video calls to confirm their identity.

Businesses, too, can benefit from updated training and protocols that emphasize the importance of verifying requests made through voice communications. In high-stakes environments, companies may consider implementing additional layers of authentication for financial transactions, such as requiring written confirmation or video verification for large payments.

Looking Ahead: The Future of AI-Driven Scams

As AI technology continues to evolve, the potential for synthetic voice scams to become even more sophisticated and widespread is a growing concern. Already, scammers are experimenting with combining voice cloning with other AI-driven tools, such as deepfake videos, to create even more convincing deceptions. It is possible that, in the near future, scammers will be able to produce not just audio but fully immersive simulations of trusted individuals, making it even harder for victims to distinguish between real and fake communications.

At the same time, efforts to combat AI-driven scams are also advancing. Governments, law enforcement agencies, and tech companies are working together to develop tools and strategies for detecting and preventing synthetic voice fraud. Biometric security measures, such as voice recognition systems, are also being refined to provide stronger defenses against voice-based attacks.

However, it is clear that the fight against AI-driven scams will require a multi-faceted approach. In addition to technological solutions, a greater emphasis on public education, legal reform, and international cooperation will be necessary to protect individuals and businesses from the rising threat of synthetic voices and other AI-enabled scams.

Conclusion

AI-generated voices have opened up a new frontier in fraud, allowing scammers to mimic trusted individuals with alarming accuracy. These scams prey on human trust and emotion, often leaving victims financially and psychologically devastated. As the technology behind synthetic voices continues to improve, the threat to individuals, businesses, and society at large will only grow. To combat this emerging form of fraud, a coordinated effort involving law enforcement, cybersecurity professionals, and public awareness campaigns will be essential. Only by staying informed and vigilant can we hope to mitigate the real and growing dangers of AI-driven scams.

Chapter 12. Fake Video Calls and Deepfakes
The Next Level of Manipulation

Introduction

In an era dominated by digital interactions, video calls have become a vital part of our personal and professional lives. From remote business meetings to virtual catch-ups with friends and family, these platforms have brought people closer, offering a sense of intimacy that text or voice calls can't match. But as with many technological advancements, the rise of video calls has opened doors for malicious actors to exploit the technology for fraudulent purposes. Coupled with the emergence of deepfake technology, a new and frightening realm of online manipulation has been born: fake video calls designed to deceive, defraud, and even emotionally exploit victims.

Understanding Fake Video Calls

At its core, a fake video call involves a fraudster presenting themselves as someone they are not. The goal is to deceive the person on the other end of the line into believing they are speaking with a trusted individual - whether it be a loved one, colleague, or figure of authority. Traditionally, fake video calls have relied on pre-recorded videos or manipulated footage to give the illusion of a live conversation. However, these tactics were often rudimentary, relying on crude editing that was easier to detect by a cautious or tech-savvy user.

Yet, as technology has advanced, so too have the methods used by fraudsters. Today's fake video calls are not merely pre-recorded snippets of conversations stitched together; they have evolved into sophisticated, real-time manipulations powered by artificial intelligence. Central to this evolution is the advent of deepfake technology, which has taken deception to an unprecedented level.

The Rise of Deepfakes: What They Are and How They Work

Deepfakes are highly realistic and often indistinguishable synthetic media created using artificial intelligence (AI) and machine learning techniques. The term "deepfake" is derived from the combination of "deep learning" and "fake", indicating the technology's reliance on deep learning algorithms to generate fraudulent images, videos, or audio. The most popular technique behind deepfakes is a type of neural network known as a Generative Adversarial Network (GAN). A GAN essentially pits two algorithms against each other - one generates fake content, while the other attempts to detect whether the content is real or fake. Over time, the system improves its ability to create realistic-looking media.

What makes deepfakes so potent is their ability to fabricate highly realistic videos where a person's face, voice, or body movements are convincingly mimicked. From a celebrity's face being placed onto another's body to creating entirely fictional conversations, deepfakes blur the line between reality and fabrication, making it increasingly difficult for the average viewer to discern between the two.

This technology has now entered the world of fake video calls, where fraudsters can impersonate almost anyone with alarming accuracy. No longer limited to pre-recorded video footage, deepfakes enable criminals to create real-time video interactions, adding a new layer of complexity and danger to online fraud.

How Deepfake Video Calls Work

Deepfake video calls take traditional fake video calls one step further by offering real-time manipulation. Using advanced software, fraudsters can map someone's face onto their own and speak with the victim in real-time. The software tracks facial movements and syncs them with the fraudulent face, creating an illusion that the person speaking is, in fact, the person being impersonated.

For example, a scammer could initiate a video call with an individual while using the likeness of their boss or colleague. With facial movements and even voice altered to resemble the person being impersonated, the victim may be tricked into believing they are having a genuine conversation. This level of interaction drastically reduces suspicion, as it replicates the nuances of face-to-face conversations - body language, facial expressions, and tone of voice.

Moreover, fraudsters can even deploy AI-driven voice mimicking software in tandem with deepfake video technology to copy the target's voice with uncanny precision. This creates a fully immersive illusion, where both the face and voice of the imposter are indistinguishable from the real person.

The Implications for Scams and Frauds

The rise of deepfake video calls has alarming implications for scams and fraud. Deepfakes bring a new level of sophistication to social engineering scams, where victims are manipulated into providing sensitive information or transferring funds. Traditional phishing techniques often rely on emails or phone calls to deceive individuals into thinking they are communicating with someone they trust. With the addition of a fake video call - where they can see and hear a trusted face - the victim's defenses are significantly lowered.

One of the most notorious applications of deepfake video calls has been in the realm of financial fraud. Imagine receiving a video call from what appears to be your bank manager, asking you to verify certain account details. Because you see and hear the person you recognize, you comply, unaware that the individual on the other side of the screen is a scammer using deepfake technology to steal your information.

Corporate espionage is another area where deepfake video calls pose a significant threat. Fraudsters may use fake video calls to gain access to sensitive business information by impersonating senior executives. By pretending to be the CEO or another high-ranking official, scammers can trick employees into divulging trade secrets, login credentials, or making unauthorized financial transactions.

Psychological Manipulation and Emotional Exploitation

Beyond financial gain, fake video calls using deepfakes have another sinister application - emotional exploitation. In some cases, fraudsters use deepfakes to impersonate loved ones and manipulate victims into making decisions that can have a lasting emotional or psychological impact.

For instance, consider a deepfake video call where a criminal impersonates a family member in distress, asking for immediate financial help. The victim, seeing the familiar face and hearing the loved one's voice, may feel compelled to act quickly without considering the possibility of fraud. This type of emotional manipulation is especially dangerous because it preys on the trust and emotional bonds between individuals, leveraging deepfakes to exploit vulnerable emotions.

Additionally, deepfake video calls can be used in romance scams, where fraudsters deceive victims into forming emotional connections with someone who does not exist. By using deepfake technology to create video evidence of a "real" person, scammers can deepen the illusion, making it harder for victims to recognize the red flags of a typical romance scam.

Deepfake and Fake Video Call Technology in Blackmail

Deepfake technology also enables a particularly nefarious type of blackmail known as "video sextortion." In these scenarios, criminals create deepfake videos of their victims, often superimposing their face onto explicit or compromising footage. The scammer then contacts the victim, threatening to release the video to the public unless a ransom is paid. Because of the realistic nature of deepfakes, victims often have difficulty proving their innocence, leaving them vulnerable to the extortionist's demands.

The rise of video-based blackmail is a terrifying evolution of older scams, which often relied on hacked emails or photographs to extract money from victims. Deepfakes provide criminals with the tools to create entirely new and damaging forms of blackmail, where individuals must contend with the possibility of having their digital likeness weaponized against them.

The Future of Deepfakes and Countermeasures

The alarming rate at which deepfake technology is advancing has prompted growing concern across industries. As deepfakes become more sophisticated, traditional methods of identifying manipulated media are becoming less effective. New AI-driven countermeasures are being developed to help detect deepfakes, including algorithms designed to identify inconsistencies in video and audio that may be invisible to the human eye. However, as detection tools improve, so too will the deepfake technology, creating a constant arms race between scammers and those working to prevent fraud.

Social media platforms, video conferencing apps, and tech companies are beginning to explore ways to incorporate deepfake detection tools into their systems. For instance, Microsoft has launched a tool that can analyze videos and provide a "deepfake confidence score", indicating the likelihood that the media has been manipulated. Similarly, Facebook and Twitter (X) are taking steps to limit the spread of deepfakes on their platforms, although these efforts are still in the early stages.

Legal frameworks are also being developed to address the rise of deepfake technology, with some governments passing laws that criminalize the use of deepfakes for malicious purposes. However, the international nature of the internet means that legal measures alone are unlikely to solve the problem. Global cooperation and technological innovation will be necessary to effectively combat the growing threat of deepfake video calls.

What Can Individuals Do to Protect Themselves?

As deepfake technology continues to evolve, individuals must take proactive steps to protect themselves from becoming victims of fake video calls. First and foremost, it is crucial to maintain a healthy level of skepticism when receiving unsolicited video calls, especially those involving sensitive information or urgent requests. If something feels off or seems too good to be true, it is always wise to double-check the identity of the caller through another channel, such as a phone call or email.

Education and awareness are also critical components of defense. By staying informed about the latest trends in deepfake and video call scams, individuals can better recognize the signs of manipulation and avoid falling prey to fraudsters. Being cautious about sharing personal information online and limiting the accessibility of private media can also reduce the risk of becoming a target for deepfake-based scams.

Conclusion

The rise of deepfake video calls represents a new and troubling frontier in the world of online fraud and manipulation. With the ability to create highly realistic and convincing digital facsimiles of people, criminals have gained a powerful tool for deceiving and exploiting victims. As deepfakes become more prevalent, the lines between truth and deception will continue to blur, making it ever more important for individuals, companies, and governments to stay vigilant and develop effective countermeasures to protect against this next level of manipulation.

Chapter 13. Blackmail via Social Media
Sextortion and Emotional Exploitation

Introduction

Social media has become an integral part of modern life, providing people with the ability to connect, share, and communicate across the globe. Platforms such as Facebook, Instagram, Twitter (X), and TikTok allow users to showcase moments of their lives, engage with others, and express their opinions. However, beneath the surface of these benefits lies a dark side that continues to grow in intensity: blackmail and sextortion. Scammers have taken advantage of the open and often anonymous nature of social media to exploit and manipulate unsuspecting users. One of the most sinister forms of this exploitation is sextortion, where victims are blackmailed using their personal content, often leading to emotional and financial devastation.

Understanding Sextortion: The Anatomy of Exploitation

Sextortion is a form of online blackmail where an individual is coerced into providing explicit images or videos, which are then used against them for financial or emotional gain. The scammer, who might pose as a romantic partner or an admirer, manipulates the victim into engaging in explicit acts, which are recorded either through fake video calls or hacked accounts. Once the material is obtained, the blackmailer threatens to release it publicly, share it with the victim's family or friends, or spread it across social media unless a ransom is paid.

In many cases, victims are lured in by what seems to be a legitimate romantic interest. Scammers often create fake profiles, using attractive pictures and convincing backstories to gain trust. As the online relationship deepens, the scammer might request a video call, during which they record intimate moments without the victim's knowledge. This manipulation often occurs gradually, starting with harmless conversations and moving into more personal and private exchanges. Once the scammer has enough compromising material, the blackmail begins.

What makes sextortion particularly terrifying is the level of emotional control the scammer gains over the victim. The threat of exposing intimate content can have a paralyzing effect, causing immense psychological distress. Victims may feel ashamed, embarrassed, or afraid to seek help, fearing judgment from others or social ostracism. This emotional manipulation often traps them in a cycle of exploitation, where they continue to meet the demands of the scammer in the hopes of avoiding exposure.

The Role of Social Media in Facilitating Sextortion

Social media plays a significant role in facilitating sextortion. The sheer scale of users on platforms such as Facebook, Instagram, and Snapchat provides an almost endless pool of potential victims. Scammers can easily create fake profiles, impersonate others, or hack into accounts to carry out their schemes. Social media platforms are designed for connection, but this very purpose makes them ripe for exploitation by those with malicious intent.

One of the most common methods used by sextortionists is impersonation. A scammer might create a fake profile, complete with photos and posts, to appear legitimate. They send friend requests or follow unsuspecting users, usually targeting individuals who seem vulnerable or isolated. After establishing a rapport, the scammer manipulates the victim into sharing explicit photos or participating in a video call.

Fake video calls have become a particularly insidious tactic in sextortion schemes. Scammers may use pre-recorded videos of attractive individuals or real-time editing software to convince victims they are engaging with someone genuine. Once the victim participates in a private or explicit conversation, the scammer captures the content and begins the process of blackmail. This tactic is highly effective because it preys on the victim's belief that they are interacting with someone they trust, only to realize too late that they have been deceived.

Hacking is another method employed by sextortionists. If a scammer can gain access to a victim's social media accounts, they can retrieve private messages, photos, and videos that can be used as leverage. Hackers may even control the victim's account, using it to contact their friends or family with threats of exposure.

The Psychological Impact of Sextortion

The emotional toll of sextortion is profound, often leading to feelings of shame, guilt, and anxiety. Victims may feel trapped, believing they have no way out of the situation without suffering personal or social consequences. Many individuals who fall victim to sextortion experience a deep sense of isolation, afraid to seek help for fear of further humiliation.

One of the most damaging aspects of sextortion is the manipulation of the victim's emotions. Scammers often exploit vulnerabilities, such as loneliness, insecurity, or a desire for connection, to gain control. Once they have established this emotional bond, they twist it into a tool for exploitation. The victim may feel betrayed, confused, and ashamed for having trusted the wrong person. This emotional exploitation can have long-lasting effects, leading to depression, anxiety, and in extreme cases, suicidal thoughts.

Victims are often caught in a vicious cycle of compliance, where they continue to meet the demands of the scammer in the hopes that the blackmail will stop. However, appeasing the blackmailer rarely resolves the situation. In many cases, the demands for money or additional explicit content only increase, further entrenching the victim in a web of control and fear. The longer the blackmail continues, the more damage is done to the victim's emotional and psychological well-being.

Financial Exploitation: The Ransom Demand

While the emotional toll of sextortion is devastating, the financial aspect is equally alarming. Scammers often demand large sums of money from their victims, threatening to release explicit content unless they are paid. In some cases, victims are forced to empty their savings, take out loans, or sell personal belongings to meet the scammer's demands.

The financial exploitation can be especially damaging for younger victims, such as teenagers or young adults, who may not have the resources to pay the ransom. For these individuals, the threat of exposure looms large, often leading them to take desperate measures to try and stop the blackmail. Unfortunately, paying the scammer rarely results in an end to the harassment. In many cases, the blackmailer will continue to demand more money, knowing that the victim is now in a vulnerable and desperate position.

What makes the financial aspect of sextortion particularly cruel is that scammers often target victims who are already vulnerable. They prey on individuals who may be experiencing financial difficulties or emotional distress, using these weaknesses to exploit them further. The combination of emotional manipulation and financial demands creates a deeply harmful situation where the victim feels powerless to escape.

The Growing Threat: Sextortion in the Digital Age

As technology advances, so do the tactics used by sextortionists. With the rise of deepfakes, scammers now have the ability to create highly convincing fake videos and images, making it even harder for victims to discern what is real and what is manipulated. Deepfake technology allows scammers to superimpose a victim's face onto explicit content, creating a video or image that appears genuine but is entirely fabricated.

This new frontier of sextortion is particularly concerning because it opens up the possibility for even greater exploitation. Victims may be blackmailed with fake content that they never participated in, yet the threat of exposure is just as real. The emotional and psychological impact of being accused of something one did not do can be as devastating as the blackmail itself.

Furthermore, the global nature of social media means that scammers can operate from anywhere in the world, making it difficult for law enforcement to track them down. Many sextortionists operate from countries with lax regulations on cybercrime, using anonymity and distance to evade capture. This international element adds another layer of complexity to the problem, making it harder for victims to find justice or recourse.

Prevention and Protection: How to Safeguard Yourself

While sextortion is a growing threat, there are steps individuals can take to protect themselves from falling victim to these schemes. Awareness is the first line of defense. Understanding the tactics used by sextortionists and being cautious about who you interact with online can help prevent exploitation. It is essential to verify the identity of anyone you engage with on social media, especially if the conversation turns personal or intimate.

Avoid sharing explicit content or engaging in private video calls with individuals you have not met in person. Once explicit material is shared, it is challenging to control where it ends up, making it easier for scammers to exploit you. Be cautious about what you post on social media, as even seemingly harmless content can be used by scammers to build a profile of you.

In the event that you are targeted by a sextortionist, it is crucial to remain calm and not give in to their demands. Contact law enforcement and report the scammer to the social media platform. Many platforms have policies in place to handle cases of sextortion, and taking swift action can help mitigate the damage. Most importantly, do not be afraid to seek help from trusted friends or family members. Emotional support can be invaluable in navigating the psychological toll of sextortion.

Conclusion: A Call for Greater Awareness

Sextortion and blackmail via social media are growing problems in the digital age, affecting countless individuals around the world. The combination of emotional exploitation, financial extortion, and the fear of exposure creates a deeply harmful experience for victims. As social media continues to evolve, so too do the tactics used by scammers, making it essential for users to remain vigilant and informed.

Addressing the issue of sextortion requires a collective effort from individuals, social media platforms, and law enforcement agencies. Increased awareness, better reporting mechanisms, and stronger regulations are needed to combat this form of online blackmail effectively. Until then, it is vital for users to protect themselves, be cautious in their online interactions, and seek help if they fall victim to these schemes.

Chapter 14. The Rise of Fake Phone Calls
Scammers on the Line

Introduction

The digital age has brought with it incredible convenience, allowing people to stay connected through various online platforms, but it has also opened the door to new forms of deception. Among these are phone-based scams, which have risen exponentially in recent years. Scammers are employing increasingly sophisticated techniques, with some even turning to artificial intelligence (AI) to create personalized, convincing narratives that trap unsuspecting victims. This chapter explores the methods used in phone scams, including AI-powered calls, and examines how scammers use data collected from social media to make their fraud more believable.

The Evolution of Phone Scams: From Simple to Sophisticated

Phone scams are not a new phenomenon. In the past, scammers would rely on simple, generic scripts to swindle unsuspecting individuals. Many people may recall calls claiming that they had won a lottery or that their credit card had been compromised. These early scams often relied on fear or greed to push victims into hastily providing personal information. However, as people became more familiar with these tactics, the effectiveness of these simple scams waned.

Enter the modern era, where technology plays a pivotal role in the evolution of phone scams. Scammers no longer rely solely on random cold-calling with generic scripts. Instead, they now use data, often harvested from social media profiles, to make their scams appear more authentic and targeted. By using personal details such as a person's name, family information, or recent activity, scammers create a façade of legitimacy, making it more difficult for victims to discern that they are being manipulated. This technique is called "social engineering", and it has significantly increased the success rate of phone-based scams.

Social Media as a Goldmine for Scammers

Social media has become a treasure trove of personal information, offering scammers the perfect tools to craft believable phone scams. Most users freely share details about their lives - birthdays, family photos, vacations, and even their work schedules. Scammers, posing as legitimate callers, use this publicly available information to make their approach appear credible.

For instance, a scammer may call posing as a family member in distress, mentioning specific details such as the family member's location or recent activities, which were likely shared on a public platform. They might claim to have been involved in an accident, stranded in a foreign country, or even held hostage. The goal is to incite panic, leading the victim to act quickly and wire money without verifying the situation.

The manipulation of social media data doesn't stop there. Scammers also use it to pose as businesses, government agencies, or even charities. They can craft elaborate narratives that seem plausible based on the victim's online activity. For instance, if someone recently tweeted about an upcoming trip, a scammer might call pretending to be from an airline or a travel insurance company, stating that there is a problem with their reservation. The level of personalization that social media affords scammers makes these fraudulent calls harder to spot and easier to fall for.

AI-Powered Phone Scams: The New Frontier of Fraud

The use of artificial intelligence has added another layer of sophistication to phone scams. AI can analyze vast amounts of data and simulate human conversations more convincingly than ever before. With advancements in AI-driven voice synthesis, scammers can now mimic the voices of real people, making it nearly impossible for victims to distinguish between a real or a fake call.

These AI-powered calls are often used in extortion schemes, where scammers mimic the voice of a loved one to demand ransom. Imagine receiving a call from what sounds like your spouse or child, begging for help and explaining that they are in grave danger. Scammers are using AI to create convincing voice models, based on short voice samples they obtain from public videos, social media platforms, or hacked data. By leveraging this technology, scammers prey on the emotional vulnerability of their victims.

AI is also used to create automated phone systems that can carry on extended conversations, adapt to a victim's responses, and maintain the illusion of legitimacy. For example, a scammer posing as a bank representative might use an AI system to verify the victim's identity by asking for sensitive personal information. If the victim hesitates, the AI can react in real time, adjusting its script to sound more convincing or reassuring. This creates an unnerving scenario where victims feel like they are speaking to a real human, making it harder for them to walk away from the scam.

The Role of Data Breaches in Enabling Phone Scams

Social media platforms are not the only source of information for phone scammers. Data breaches are another key factor in the rise of sophisticated phone scams. When large companies experience data breaches, vast amounts of sensitive information - including names, phone numbers, email addresses, and even social security numbers - are exposed to criminals. Scammers can then use this information to initiate targeted attacks via phone calls.

In one notorious example, a healthcare company experienced a data breach that exposed the personal information of millions of customers. Scammers quickly took advantage, calling victims and posing as representatives from the healthcare provider. Using the stolen data, they were able to confirm basic details such as the victim's name, policy number, and even recent medical visits. This level of specificity made the scam almost indistinguishable from a legitimate call, and many victims fell prey to it, providing additional sensitive information or paying fake fees.

As more data breaches occur, the pool of information available to scammers continues to grow, enabling them to refine their techniques and make their scams even more targeted and effective.

Common Phone Scam Tactics

While AI and data breaches have added new dimensions to phone scams, many of the tactics remain rooted in the same psychological manipulation techniques that scammers have used for decades. Understanding these tactics can help individuals recognize when they are being targeted by a phone scam.

1. Impersonation of Authority Figures: Scammers often pose as government officials, law enforcement officers, or representatives from financial institutions. They create a sense of urgency, claiming that there is a serious problem - such as unpaid taxes, a warrant for arrest, or a frozen bank account - and pressure the victim into providing sensitive information or making payments. By leveraging the authority of these institutions, scammers create fear and confusion, which makes victims more likely to comply.

2. Family Emergency Scams: These scams play on a victim's love and concern for their family. A scammer may pose as a family member or a friend in distress, claiming that they need immediate financial help due to an emergency. As mentioned earlier, scammers often use social media to gather personal details that make their story more believable.

3. Tech Support Scams: In these cases, scammers pose as tech support representatives from well-known companies like Microsoft or Apple. They claim that the victim's computer has been infected with malware or that there is a serious security issue. The scammer then convinces the victim to grant remote access to their computer, where they can steal personal information or install malicious software.

4. Prize and Lottery Scams: These scams lure victims with the promise of winning a large sum of money or valuable prizes. However, in order to claim the prize, the victim is told they must first pay a processing fee or provide personal information. Once the victim complies, the scammer disappears, and the prize is never received.

5. Caller ID Spoofing: A common tactic that enhances the effectiveness of phone scams is caller ID spoofing, where

scammers manipulate the information displayed on the recipient's phone. They may make it appear as though the call is coming from a legitimate source, such as a local government office, a trusted business, or even the victim's own phone number. This technique makes it more difficult for individuals to discern whether the call is fraudulent, especially when combined with personalized information from social media or data breaches.

The Financial and Emotional Impact of Phone Scams

Phone scams can have devastating financial and emotional consequences. Victims of phone-based scams often lose substantial amounts of money, which is rarely recovered. In some cases, scammers drain victims' bank accounts or steal their identities, leading to long-term financial damage. Elderly individuals, in particular, are frequent targets of phone scams due to their perceived vulnerability and unfamiliarity with modern technology.

The emotional toll of phone scams can be equally damaging. Victims often feel ashamed, embarrassed, and violated after falling for a scam, and the sense of betrayal can linger long after the financial loss is addressed. In family emergency scams, the emotional distress is magnified when victims believe a loved one is in danger, only to later discover that they were manipulated.

Combating Phone Scams: Awareness and Prevention

Awareness is the most powerful tool in combating phone scams. As scammers become more sophisticated, individuals must become more vigilant. It is essential to educate the public about common phone scam tactics and the dangers of sharing personal information online. Social media platforms should encourage users to review their privacy settings and limit the amount of personal information they share publicly.

Governments and businesses also play a critical role in addressing the rise of phone scams. Regulations that require phone companies to implement stronger caller ID verification measures could help reduce the effectiveness of caller ID spoofing. Furthermore, businesses should invest in robust cybersecurity practices to prevent data breaches that provide scammers with the personal information needed to carry out their schemes.

In the digital age, phone scams are an ever-present threat. While technology has enabled scammers to become more effective and elusive, it has also given individuals the tools to protect themselves. By staying informed, exercising caution, and reporting fraudulent calls, individuals can help curb the rise of fake phone calls and protect themselves from becoming victims of these increasingly sophisticated scams.

Chapter 15. Financial Scams and Cryptocurrency Fraud

Introduction

In the digital age, financial scams have evolved in both complexity and reach, and one of the most significant contributors to this evolution has been the rise of cryptocurrency. Cryptocurrency, with its decentralized and often anonymous nature, has created a fertile ground for scammers to exploit unsuspecting individuals. While it offers legitimate opportunities for investment and transactions, it has also become synonymous with fraud and deceit, particularly through platforms like social media where users are targeted en masse. This article delves into the various financial scams associated with cryptocurrency fraud, how they operate, and the steps individuals can take to protect themselves.

The Rise of Cryptocurrency and Its Appeal to Scammers

Cryptocurrency emerged as an alternative to traditional banking, heralded for its transparency, security, and freedom from centralized control. Bitcoin, the first and most well-known cryptocurrency, debuted in 2009 and opened a new frontier in digital finance. Since then, the cryptocurrency market has exploded, with thousands of new currencies like Ethereum, Litecoin, and Chainlink gaining popularity.

However, the very attributes that make cryptocurrency attractive to users - such as anonymity, decentralization, and irreversible transactions - also appeal to scammers.

Unlike traditional financial systems where authorities can freeze accounts or trace transactions, cryptocurrency transactions are harder to track, and once funds are sent, they are often unrecoverable.

Moreover, the general lack of regulation in the crypto space has left loopholes for fraudsters to exploit. In many jurisdictions, cryptocurrencies exist in a legal gray area, meaning law enforcement agencies may have limited power to intervene in cases of fraud. This lack of oversight combined with the allure of quick profits has made cryptocurrency a prime target for financial scams.

Types of Cryptocurrency Scams

Cryptocurrency fraud can take many forms, each preying on different vulnerabilities of the target audience. Below are some of the most common types of cryptocurrency scams.

1. Fake Investment Platforms

One of the most prevalent forms of cryptocurrency fraud involves fake investment platforms that promise high returns on investment with little to no risk. These platforms are often advertised aggressively on social media, with scammers posing as successful investors, influencers, or even celebrities to lure victims.

Once individuals invest their money, they may initially see their balance grow, convincing them that the platform is legitimate. However, when they attempt to withdraw their funds, they either find that the withdrawal process is indefinitely delayed or that their account has been closed entirely. By the time victims realize they've been scammed, the fraudsters have already disappeared with their money.

2. Ponzi and Pyramid Schemes

Ponzi and pyramid schemes have found new life in the world of cryptocurrency. In these scams, fraudsters recruit new investors and use their money to pay off earlier investors, creating the illusion of a profitable investment. As more people invest, the scam grows, and the returns for early participants create the impression that the scheme is legitimate.

However, such schemes are unsustainable and eventually collapse when the scammer is no longer able to recruit new investors. By the time the scheme falls apart, the scammer has made off with substantial sums of money, leaving later investors with significant losses.

A famous example is the "Bitconnect" Ponzi scheme, which promised investors guaranteed high returns but collapsed in 2018, costing investors over $2 billion.

3. Pump-and-Dump Schemes

In a pump-and-dump scheme, fraudsters artificially inflate the price of a low-value cryptocurrency by spreading misleading or false information, often through social media channels or online forums. The goal is to create a sense of FOMO (fear of missing out) among investors, leading them to buy the cryptocurrency at inflated prices.

Once the price reaches a peak, the fraudsters sell off their holdings, causing the price to crash. The investors who bought in during the "pump" phase are left with devalued assets, while the scammers walk away with substantial profits. Such schemes are often orchestrated by anonymous groups or individuals, making it difficult for victims to seek recourse.

4. Rug Pull Scams

A "rug pull" occurs when the creators of a new cryptocurrency or decentralized finance (DeFi) project suddenly withdraw all the liquidity, leaving investors with worthless tokens. Rug pulls are particularly prevalent in the DeFi space, where new tokens are often launched with great fanfare, promising innovative features and high returns.

Scammers use social media platforms like Twitter (X), Telegram, and Reddit to hype up the project, encouraging investors to buy tokens early. Once enough people have invested, the creators withdraw the funds, causing the token's value to plummet to zero. Rug pulls have resulted in millions of dollars in losses for investors, and because the perpetrators are often anonymous, legal recourse is difficult to pursue.

5. Phishing Attacks

Phishing scams are not new, but they have adapted to the world of cryptocurrency. In a typical phishing attack, scammers send emails or messages that appear to come from legitimate cryptocurrency exchanges, wallet providers, or service platforms. These messages often contain a link that directs the victim to a fake website designed to steal their login credentials or private keys.

Once the victim enters their information, the scammers use it to access the victim's cryptocurrency wallet and transfer the funds to their own accounts. Because cryptocurrency transactions are irreversible, victims are unlikely to recover their stolen assets.

6. Fake Initial Coin Offerings (ICOs)

Initial Coin Offerings (ICOs) were a popular method for startups to raise capital by selling their own cryptocurrency tokens in exchange for established cryptocurrencies like Bitcoin or Ethereum. While many legitimate companies have raised funds through ICOs, the lack of regulation has made them a hotbed for scams.

In a fake ICO scam, fraudsters create a convincing-looking website and whitepaper that outline a fictitious project. They may even produce fake endorsements from industry experts or celebrities to bolster credibility. Once investors contribute their funds, the scammers disappear, leaving investors with worthless tokens or no tokens at all.

The Role of Social Media in Cryptocurrency Scams

Social media has become a powerful tool for cryptocurrency scammers. Platforms like Facebook, Twitter (X), Instagram, and YouTube are ideal for fraudsters to reach large audiences with minimal effort and cost. Social media ads, influencer endorsements, and viral posts can quickly create buzz around fraudulent schemes, making them appear legitimate.

One of the most common tactics used by scammers on social media is impersonation. Fraudsters create fake profiles of well-known figures, such as CEOs of cryptocurrency companies, financial experts, or even celebrities, and use these profiles to promote investment schemes. They often claim to be giving away cryptocurrency in exchange for a smaller deposit, promising that they will return a larger sum. These scams are particularly effective because they play on people's trust in familiar public figures.

Cryptocurrency giveaways on platforms like Twitter (X) have become notorious for being fraudulent. Scammers will ask individuals to send a small amount of cryptocurrency to a given address, with the promise of sending back double or triple the amount. Of course, once the individual sends their funds, they never see them again.

The Impact of Cryptocurrency Fraud on Victims

The financial losses associated with cryptocurrency fraud can be devastating. Because of the decentralized and largely unregulated nature of cryptocurrencies, recovering lost funds is often impossible. Victims may also experience psychological and emotional distress, especially if they had invested significant sums of money or were relying on cryptocurrency gains for financial stability.

Moreover, the anonymity of scammers makes it difficult to track them down and hold them accountable. In many cases, victims have no recourse but to accept their losses, which can erode trust in legitimate cryptocurrency platforms and the broader financial system.

How to Protect Yourself from Cryptocurrency Scams

While cryptocurrency fraud is rampant, there are steps individuals can take to protect themselves from falling victim.

1. Research thoroughly: **Before investing in any cryptocurrency or related platform, conduct thorough research. Check for reviews, verify the legitimacy of the

project, and look out for red flags such as promises of guaranteed returns or pressure to invest quickly.

2. Be wary of unsolicited offers: If you receive an unsolicited offer to invest in cryptocurrency or participate in a giveaway, proceed with caution. Scammers often use these tactics to lure victims into fraudulent schemes.

3. Use reputable exchanges and wallets: Stick to well-known and reputable cryptocurrency exchanges and wallet providers. Avoid downloading wallet apps or accessing exchanges through links in emails or social media posts.

4. Enable two-factor authentication (2FA): Protect your cryptocurrency accounts by enabling two-factor authentication. This adds an extra layer of security, making it harder for scammers to access your accounts.

5. Beware of phishing attacks: Be cautious when receiving emails or messages claiming to be from cryptocurrency exchanges or wallets. Always verify the sender's identity and avoid clicking on suspicious links.

Conclusion

As cryptocurrency continues to grow in popularity, so too do the opportunities for scammers to exploit unsuspecting individuals. Financial scams and cryptocurrency fraud are becoming increasingly sophisticated, often using social media to reach and deceive victims. While the decentralized and anonymous nature of cryptocurrency can offer benefits, it also presents significant risks.

By staying informed and vigilant, individuals can reduce their chances of falling victim to cryptocurrency fraud. Understanding the tactics used by scammers and taking proactive steps to safeguard one's investments is crucial in navigating the complex and often perilous world of digital finance.

Chapter 16. Social Media Ad Scams
Clickbait and Fraudulent Offers

Introduction

In today's digital age, social media platforms like Instagram and Facebook have become an essential part of daily life for millions worldwide. They are not only used for sharing personal updates, photos, and videos but have also emerged as powerful tools for marketing and advertising. While legitimate businesses leverage these platforms to connect with consumers, unscrupulous actors exploit the same tools to scam unsuspecting users. Social media ad scams, particularly clickbait and fraudulent offers, have become a pervasive problem. This article explores the deceptive practices used in social media advertising, the harm they cause, and ways users can protect themselves.

The Rise of Social Media Ad Scams

Social media platforms have millions of active users, making them fertile ground for businesses and individuals to advertise products and services. However, this massive audience also attracts cybercriminals who exploit users' trust and the fast-paced nature of social media. One of the most common forms of social media fraud is the advertisement scam, which often appears in the form of clickbait or fraudulent offers.

Clickbait refers to sensationalized and misleading headlines or thumbnails designed to attract users' attention, encouraging them to click on a link or ad. These ads often promise too-good-to-be-true deals, such as high-quality products at drastically reduced prices or exclusive offers that seem irresistible. Upon clicking, users are usually directed to websites that sell counterfeit goods, harvest personal data, or infect their devices with malware.

Fraudulent offers, on the other hand, are disguised as legitimate deals but are designed to trick users into spending money on products or services that either don't exist or are of extremely poor quality. These offers often come from seemingly reputable brands or stores, luring users in with limited-time promotions, free giveaways, or deep discounts. In reality, they are fraudulent schemes aimed at scamming consumers out of their money or personal information.

Types of Social Media Ad Scams

1. Clickbait Ads

Clickbait ads are designed to generate clicks, and they often do so by employing manipulative tactics. For instance, a user scrolling through Instagram might see an ad with a sensational headline like "This Simple Trick Will Change Your Life" or "Doctors Hate This New Health Supplement". These headlines play on curiosity, fear, or excitement to lure users into clicking the ad. The promise of life-changing information or an unbelievable deal is often irresistible, but the destination website is rarely as promised.

These clickbait ads often lead to websites filled with fake testimonials, exaggerated claims, and pressure tactics that encourage the user to make an impulsive purchase. Worse, some clickbait ads are designed to collect personal data, such as credit card information, without delivering any tangible product. In some cases, users may be directed to phishing websites that mirror legitimate sites, where they inadvertently provide sensitive information to scammers.

2. Fake Product Ads

Fraudulent offers in social media ads often involve fake products or counterfeit goods. These ads frequently promise high-end items, such as designer handbags, electronics, or luxury cosmetics, at unbelievably low prices. The product images may look genuine, and the website may appear professional, but the product itself is either non-existent or of extremely poor quality.

For example, a user may come across a Facebook ad offering a "50% off" sale on popular branded sneakers. When they click on the ad and make a purchase, they either receive a counterfeit product or nothing at all. The scammer, meanwhile, pockets the money and disappears, leaving the consumer with no recourse for refunds or customer support.

3. Subscription Traps

Another common scam involves subscription traps, where users are enticed to sign up for a "free trial" of a product or service, only to find themselves unknowingly enrolled in a costly subscription service. These scams are often promoted via ads for beauty products, weight loss supplements, or other wellness items. The ad might claim, "Try Our Product for Free – Just Pay Shipping!" However, hidden in the fine print is a clause that automatically enrolls the user in a subscription, charging them a recurring fee.

Consumers may not realize they have been signed up for a subscription until they start noticing unexpected charges on their credit card. By the time they try to cancel, it is often too late, and they may have already lost a significant amount of money.

4. Charity Scams

In addition to fraudulent product offers, social media is also rife with fake charity scams. Scammers exploit users' goodwill, particularly during times of crisis or natural disasters, by creating fake charity pages or running ads that solicit donations for a seemingly good cause. Users who want to help those in need may be drawn to these ads, believing their money will go to a reputable charity. However, instead of aiding victims, the funds go directly into the scammer's pocket.

5. Investment and Get-Rich-Quick Schemes

Social media ad scams are not limited to physical products. Many scammers also promote fake investment opportunities or get-rich-quick schemes, capitalizing on users' desire for financial independence or wealth. These ads often promise high returns with little to no risk, using language like "Make $10,000 a Month from Home" or "Double Your Money in 30 Days".

In reality, these schemes are often Ponzi or pyramid schemes, where the scammer takes money from new investors to pay earlier investors, eventually collapsing and leaving most people with nothing. Cryptocurrency and forex trading scams have also proliferated on social media, with scammers presenting themselves as successful traders who can help users get rich quickly.

Why Social Media Ad Scams Are So Effective

Social media ad scams are particularly effective because they exploit the trust that users place in the platforms and the speed at which content is consumed. On platforms like Instagram and Facebook, users are constantly scrolling through their feeds, engaging with content in a matter of seconds. This fast-paced environment means that users are more likely to click on an enticing ad without thoroughly vetting its legitimacy.

Additionally, social media platforms often personalize ads based on users' interests, location, and browsing history. Scammers take advantage of this by crafting ads that seem highly relevant to the user. For example, someone who recently searched for workout gear might be shown an ad for discounted fitness products. The user, trusting the ad's relevance to their recent search, may be more inclined to click and make a purchase without realizing it's a scam.

Another reason these scams are so successful is the anonymity provided by social media. Scammers can easily create fake business pages or run ads under false names, making it difficult for users to verify the legitimacy of the offer. Furthermore, social media platforms often lack stringent vetting processes for advertisers, allowing scammers to run ads without undergoing significant scrutiny.

The Consequences of Falling for Social Media Ad Scams

The consequences of falling for a social media ad scam can be devastating, both financially and emotionally. Victims of these scams may lose hundreds or even thousands of dollars, with little to no recourse for getting their money back. In addition to financial losses, victims may also have their personal information, such as credit card details or home addresses, stolen. This can lead to further crimes, such as identity theft or credit card fraud.

Moreover, the emotional toll of being scammed can be significant. Victims often feel embarrassed, ashamed, or violated, especially if they had trusted the platform where the scam took place. Many people are reluctant to report these incidents because they fear judgment or believe they will not be taken seriously.

How to Protect Yourself from Social Media Ad Scams

Although social media ad scams are prevalent, there are steps users can take to protect themselves. First and foremost, it's essential to approach all ads with caution. If an offer seems too good to be true, it probably is. Always research the company or product before making a purchase, and look for reviews or complaints online. Legitimate businesses will often have a history of satisfied customers, while scams will usually have negative reviews or no online presence at all.

Another key protection measure is to avoid clicking on suspicious ads. If an ad uses sensationalized language, promises unrealistic results, or pressures you to act quickly, it's likely a scam. Instead of clicking on the ad, search for the product or company directly on a trusted platform.

Users should also be wary of ads that ask for personal information upfront. Legitimate companies will not request sensitive information like credit card details or Social Security numbers through social media ads. If an ad asks for this information, it's best to close the page immediately.

Finally, it's important to report any suspicious ads to the social media platform. Both Instagram and Facebook have mechanisms in place for users to report fraudulent ads, and doing so helps protect other users from falling victim to the same scams. By reporting these scams, users can play an active role in making social media a safer place for everyone.

Conclusion

Social media ad scams, including clickbait and fraudulent offers, are a growing concern in today's digital landscape. As social media platforms continue to play a significant role in how people interact with brands, it's crucial for users to remain vigilant. By understanding the tactics scammers use and knowing how to protect themselves, users can avoid falling victim to these schemes and make more informed decisions online.

Chapter 17. Marketplace Scams
Fake Products and Services

Introduction

In the fast-paced digital age, online marketplaces have become a convenient platform for consumers worldwide to purchase everything from electronics to clothing, furniture, and services. However, with this convenience comes an array of risks, as fraudulent activities have also migrated to these digital spaces. Marketplace scams, particularly those involving fake products and services, have surged as scammers take advantage of the anonymity and reach provided by the internet. This chapter delves into the various forms of marketplace scams, examining how scammers operate, the impact on victims, and steps consumers can take to avoid falling prey to these deceitful tactics.

The Evolution of Marketplace Scams

The rise of e-commerce platforms like Amazon, eBay, and Etsy, as well as classified ad sites like Craigslist and Facebook Marketplace, has revolutionized the shopping experience. These platforms provide users with an opportunity to buy and sell goods with ease, often from independent sellers or small businesses. However, this convenience comes at a price, as these marketplaces are also fertile ground for fraudulent activities. Scammers use these platforms to sell counterfeit goods, offer non-existent services, and engage in schemes that deceive and exploit unsuspecting buyers.

As online shopping has grown, so too has the complexity of scams targeting these marketplaces. Initially, marketplace scams were relatively simple, involving fake listings or duplicate products. Today, scammers use more sophisticated tactics such as cloning legitimate seller profiles, manipulating product reviews, and even creating entire fake storefronts that appear credible to unsuspecting buyers. This evolution has made it increasingly difficult for consumers to distinguish between legitimate sellers and fraudulent ones.

Types of Marketplace Scams

There are several types of marketplace scams that consumers may encounter. These scams typically fall into two broad categories: fake products and fake services. Each category carries its own set of risks, but both can cause significant financial and emotional harm to victims.

1. Fake Products

Fake product scams are among the most common forms of marketplace fraud. Scammers often create listings for high-demand items such as electronics, luxury goods, or designer clothing, offering them at a fraction of the retail price. However, the products delivered to consumers are often counterfeit, substandard, or never delivered at all.

Counterfeit Goods

Counterfeit goods are a pervasive problem on online marketplaces. These fake products are designed to look like legitimate items from well-known brands but are often of inferior quality. Luxury goods such as handbags, watches, and shoes are particularly susceptible to counterfeiting. Scammers prey on buyers looking for bargains, offering these counterfeit goods at prices that seem too good to be true.

One common tactic used by scammers is to steal images and descriptions from legitimate sellers. The fraudulent listings may appear professional and convincing, but the product delivered (if delivered at all) is often a cheap imitation. Victims may not realize they have been scammed until they receive the product, by which point the scammer has often vanished, leaving them with little recourse for recovering their money.

Non-Existent Products

In some cases, scammers list products that do not exist. They create fake listings for popular items, collect payments from buyers, and then disappear without sending anything. These scams are particularly common for high-demand products like new smartphones, gaming consoles, and concert tickets, where buyers may feel pressured to act quickly to secure a good deal.

Scammers may offer these non-existent products at a discounted rate to lure buyers into a sense of urgency. Once the buyer has transferred the payment, the seller may provide false shipping information or simply stop responding to messages, leaving the buyer with no product and no way to recover their money.

Knockoff or Substandard Products

Another type of fake product scam involves the sale of knockoff or substandard goods that are passed off as genuine. For example, a scammer may list a product as being from a reputable brand but deliver a cheap knockoff that does not meet the buyer's expectations. These scams can be particularly harmful in cases where the products are unsafe, such as counterfeit electronics or beauty products that do not meet safety standards.

Knockoff products can be difficult to identify in online listings, as scammers often use stolen images and descriptions to make their listings appear legitimate. Buyers may only realize they have been scammed when they receive the product and notice its poor quality or performance.

2. Fake Services

Fake service scams are another prevalent form of marketplace fraud. In these scams, scammers offer services such as home repairs, cleaning, or freelance work but fail to deliver on their promises. These scams often target individuals who are seeking affordable services or those in urgent need of assistance.

Non-Existent Services

In some cases, scammers create fake listings for services that do not exist. For example, a scammer may pose as a contractor or service provider and offer services such as plumbing, electrical work, or landscaping. Once the buyer pays a deposit or upfront fee, the scammer disappears without delivering the service. Victims of these scams may be left without the promised service and out of pocket for the payment they made.

These scams can be particularly harmful for individuals in urgent situations, such as those in need of emergency home repairs. Scammers prey on the vulnerability of these individuals, offering services at a discounted rate or promising quick results to gain their trust.

Fake Freelancers

Freelance work platforms like Upwork and Fiverr have also become breeding grounds for fake service scams. Scammers may pose as freelancers offering graphic design, writing, programming, or other services, only to deliver substandard work or fail to deliver anything at all. These scams are often difficult to detect, as the scammers may use fake portfolios or reviews to build credibility.

In some cases, fake freelancers may ask for payment upfront, promising quick turnaround times. However, once the payment is made, the quality of the work may be poor, or the freelancer may stop communicating altogether. Victims of these scams may be left with unfinished projects and lost funds.

The Impact of Marketplace Scams on Consumers

The impact of marketplace scams can be significant, both financially and emotionally. Victims of these scams often lose money, either by paying for a product or service that is never delivered or by receiving a counterfeit or substandard item. In some cases, the financial losses can be substantial, particularly for individuals who purchase high-value items or services.

Beyond the financial harm, marketplace scams can also take an emotional toll on victims. Many individuals feel violated or embarrassed after being scammed, particularly if they trusted the seller or believed they were getting a good deal. The sense of betrayal and helplessness that often accompanies these scams can leave victims feeling vulnerable and hesitant to trust online marketplaces in the future.

Additionally, marketplace scams can erode consumer confidence in online shopping as a whole. As stories of fake products and services become more widespread, potential buyers may become wary of using online marketplaces, fearing they will fall victim to a scam. This hesitancy can have a broader impact on the e-commerce industry, reducing sales and hindering the growth of legitimate businesses that rely on these platforms.

How Scammers Operate

Scammers operating on online marketplaces use a variety of tactics to deceive their victims. One common method is to create fake seller profiles or clone legitimate ones, making it appear as though they are trustworthy sellers with positive reviews. By doing so, they exploit the credibility of the platform and the trust consumers place in it.

Another tactic used by scammers is to manipulate product reviews. They may create fake reviews or pay for positive feedback to make their listings appear more legitimate. In some cases, scammers may even send cheap products to random individuals to generate "verified purchase" reviews, further boosting the credibility of their listings.

Scammers also take advantage of the anonymity provided by online marketplaces. Many platforms allow sellers to use pseudonyms or remain anonymous, making it difficult for buyers to verify their identities. Additionally, scammers may use multiple accounts or change their usernames frequently to avoid detection by the platform's security measures.

Preventing Marketplace Scams

While marketplace scams are pervasive, there are steps consumers can take to protect themselves from falling victim to these fraudulent schemes. One of the most important precautions is to research the seller before making a purchase. Buyers should check the seller's profile, read reviews from other buyers, and verify that the product or service being offered is legitimate.

Consumers should also be wary of deals that seem too good to be true. Scammers often lure buyers with low prices or limited-time offers, creating a sense of urgency that pushes individuals to make hasty decisions. It is essential to remain cautious and avoid rushing into purchases without verifying the legitimacy of the seller or product.

Another effective way to prevent marketplace scams is to use secure payment methods. Many online marketplaces offer buyer protection programs that allow consumers to dispute transactions and recover their funds if they are scammed. Buyers should avoid paying for products or services using direct bank transfers or other methods that offer no recourse for recovering their money.

Conclusion

Marketplace scams involving fake products and services are a growing threat in the digital age. As online shopping continues to expand, scammers are finding new and innovative ways to exploit consumers, often leaving them with financial losses and emotional distress. By understanding the tactics used by scammers and taking steps to protect themselves, consumers can reduce the risk of falling victim to these fraudulent schemes. However, it is essential for online marketplaces to continue improving their security measures and buyer protection programs to ensure a safe and trustworthy shopping experience for all.

Chapter 18. Combating Social Media Fraud
Awareness, Prevention, and Recovery

Introduction

As social media platforms have evolved, so have the strategies used by fraudsters. While platforms like Facebook, Instagram, and Twitter (X) offer unparalleled opportunities for communication and community building, they also provide fertile ground for fraudulent activities. The previous chapters of this book have explored the wide variety of scams that pervade the digital world - from romance scams and phishing attacks to fake video calls and cryptocurrency fraud. In this final chapter, we will focus on actionable steps that can be taken to combat social media fraud, covering key areas such as raising awareness, adopting preventive measures, and recovering from online scams.

Understanding the Landscape: Awareness is Key

The first and most critical step in combating social media fraud is awareness. Most victims of fraud fall prey because they are unaware of how these scams operate or how convincing they can be. It is important to understand that fraudsters take advantage of the very nature of social media: trust and connectivity. By exploiting personal information shared on these platforms, scammers are able to construct highly targeted and convincing schemes.

There are three primary ways fraud manifests on social media: identity theft, financial fraud, and emotional manipulation. These often work in combination. For example, a romance scam may start as emotional manipulation but can quickly evolve into financial fraud once the scammer gains the victim's trust. By raising awareness of these tactics, users are better equipped to recognize red flags.

Common Tactics Used by Scammers

Before diving into prevention strategies, it is essential to revisit some common tactics employed by fraudsters. Scammers often use fake profiles, phishing links, deepfake videos, and fabricated endorsements to lure victims. They may impersonate high-profile individuals, use AI-generated voices to make phone calls seem legitimate, or send private messages designed to provoke an emotional response. Understanding these tactics makes it easier to spot fraudulent behavior early on.

Some social media platforms have taken steps to educate users on common fraud schemes, but much of the responsibility falls on individuals to protect themselves. Keeping up with trends in online scams is crucial, as fraudsters continuously adapt their methods in response to new technologies and security measures.

Prevention: Protecting Yourself and Others

Prevention begins with a robust digital hygiene routine. By adopting simple but effective habits, users can significantly reduce the likelihood of falling victim to fraud. Here are some key preventive measures:

1. Strengthening Account Security

One of the most effective ways to prevent social media fraud is by securing your accounts. Use strong, unique passwords for each platform, and enable two-factor authentication (2FA) whenever possible. 2FA adds an additional layer of security by requiring users to provide two forms of verification - usually something they know (like a password) and something they have (like a text message code). If a scammer attempts to gain access to your account, 2FA makes it much more difficult for them to succeed.

Regularly updating your passwords and using password managers can also help protect against account takeover. Many people use the same password across multiple platforms, making it easier for scammers to compromise several accounts at once. Avoid this practice, and make sure your passwords are complex and difficult to guess.

2. Scrutinizing Friend Requests and Messages

Fraudsters often use fake profiles to send friend requests or direct messages to potential victims. Before accepting a friend request from someone you don't know, take a moment to review their profile. Is it newly created? Does it have only a few followers or connections? Are there inconsistencies in the photos or information? These can all be signs of a fake account.

Similarly, be wary of unsolicited messages, particularly those that contain links or ask for personal information. Scammers frequently use social engineering techniques to manipulate people into clicking on malicious links or divulging sensitive information. If you receive a message that seems suspicious, do not click on any links, and report the account to the platform's moderation team.

3. Verifying Influencers and Endorsements

With influencer marketing becoming increasingly prevalent, many users rely on endorsements from social media personalities to make purchasing decisions. Unfortunately, not all influencers are trustworthy. Some may promote products or services that are part of a scam, or worse, they may have inflated their follower count with fake accounts to appear more influential than they are.

Before making a purchase based on an influencer's recommendation, do some research. Check for legitimate reviews from other users, and verify the authenticity of the influencer's following. Tools like Social Blade can be used to analyze the growth patterns of an influencer's account, helping to identify suspicious spikes in followers or engagement.

4. Being Cautious with Online Marketplaces

Platforms like Facebook Marketplace and Instagram Shops have made it easier for scammers to sell counterfeit goods or products that don't exist. To protect yourself when making online purchases, only buy from verified sellers or reputable companies. If a deal seems too good to be true, it probably is. Always read reviews and confirm that the seller has a track record of fulfilling orders. Use secure payment methods, like credit cards or PayPal, which offer buyer protection in case something goes wrong.

Recognizing Red Flags

Even with the best preventive measures in place, it's still possible to encounter fraud on social media. Therefore, it's important to know the warning signs. Some red flags include:

Unsolicited Messages or Links: **If someone you don't know sends you a link or asks for personal information, proceed with caution. Phishing attempts are common, and** scammers often impersonate someone you know to trick you.

Requests for Money: Be suspicious of anyone who asks for money over social media, especially if it's for something urgent, like a medical emergency or a time-sensitive investment opportunity.

Too-Good-To-Be-True Offers: If an offer seems outrageously good - such as winning a prize you didn't enter for, or getting a significant discount on an expensive item - it's likely a scam.

Pressure to Act Quickly: Scammers often use urgency as a tactic to make victims act without thinking. If you feel pressured to make a quick decision, take a step back and evaluate the situation.

Recovering from Social Media Fraud

Unfortunately, even the most diligent users can fall victim to social media fraud. If you find yourself in this situation, it's crucial to act quickly to mitigate the damage. Here's what to do if you've been scammed:

1. Report the Scam

Most social media platforms have built-in tools for reporting suspicious activity, fake profiles, and phishing attempts. Reporting the scam not only helps protect you but also alerts the platform to the presence of fraud, potentially preventing others from falling victim.

Additionally, if your personal information was compromised, report the incident to the appropriate authorities. In the case of identity theft, contact your local consumer protection agency or financial institution to freeze your accounts and prevent further fraudulent transactions.

2. Secure Your Accounts

If your account has been hacked or compromised, the first step is to change your passwords and enable two-factor authentication. If you are locked out of your account, reach out to the platform's support team to regain access. Most platforms have procedures in place for recovering hacked accounts.

3. Monitor Financial Transactions

If financial information was involved in the scam, keep a close eye on your bank accounts and credit reports for any suspicious activity. If necessary, place a fraud alert on your credit file to prevent further damage. In the case of fraudulent charges, many banks offer fraud protection and may be able to reverse unauthorized transactions.

4. Educate and Warn Others

Finally, it's essential to warn others about the scam to prevent it from spreading. Sharing your experience on social media or writing a review on a scam reporting website can help others avoid the same trap.

Conclusion: Equipping Yourself for the Future

Combating social media fraud requires a multi-pronged approach: awareness, prevention, and recovery. By staying informed about the latest tactics used by scammers, strengthening your account security, and being cautious with unsolicited messages and offers, you can significantly reduce your risk of falling victim to fraud. In the unfortunate event that you are scammed, swift action - such as reporting the incident, securing your accounts, and monitoring financial activity - can help minimize the damage.

The digital world is constantly evolving, and so too are the methods of online fraudsters. But with the right tools and strategies, individuals can protect themselves and their loved ones from these ever-present threats. Staying vigilant, adopting best practices for online safety, and supporting each other in the fight against social media fraud will ultimately make the internet a safer space for everyone.

Other Books by the Author

- Groundwater Assessment and Modelling
- Water Resources Assessment, Modelling and Management
- Hydrology and Water Resources: A Comprehensive Questions and Answers Guide
- Advanced Insights in Hydrology and Water Resources
- Spirituality in Daily Life
- Spiritual Healing Techniques
- Energy Healing for Overall Wellness
- Empowered Living: Practical Solutions for Real-World Problems
- Awakening Your Inner Self: Lessons from BK Sister Shivani's Inspirational Talks
- Social Media Madness: How to Maintain Your Sanity in a Digital World
- Journey Within: 101 Spiritual Questions and Answers
- Empowered Women, Empowered World
- Social Media Security: Protecting Your Digital Life
- The Path to Peace: Overcoming Corruption, Violence, and Hatred in Our World
- Breaking the Silence: Understanding and Overcoming Sexual Violence
- Unleashing Creativity with ChatGPT: A Writing Prompt Companion
- A Comprehensive Overview of Global Challenges
- Mastering Content Creation with ChatGPT
- A Comprehensive Guide to Investment Opportunities
- Awakening Inner Light: Wisdom from the Teachings of Brahma Kumaris
- Awakening: The Path to Transformation and Divine Union
- Navigating Life's Challenges: Strategies for Success and Well-being
- Social Impact of Mobile Phones in the Digital Age
- A Guide to Resolving Family Conflicts
- Empower Yourself Against Cyber Crimes and Frauds

- Understanding Suicide: Prevention, Awareness, and Moving Forward
- Bridging Boundaries: Love and Inter-Caste Marriages in the Indian Subcontinent
- Roots Apart: Navigating Life When Children Settle Abroad
- Beyond Traditional Marriage: Navigating Live-in Relationships
- Facing the Challenges of Aging with Grace
- Empowering Single Mothers on their Journey
- Exploring the Complexities of Mother-in-Law, Daughter-in-Law Relationships
- Beyond Betrayal: Understanding and Healing from Infidelity
- Resolving Property Disputes in Indian Families
- Effective Approaches for Dealing with Teenage Behavior
- A Comprehensive Guide to Human Sexuality
- A Comprehensive Guide to a Happy, Peaceful, Healthy, and Abundant Life
- Spiritual Insights: Learning from the Great Masters
- Guide to Home Remedies for Health and Wellness
- The Complete Guide to Child Development and Care
- Safeguarding Against Scams and Frauds in the Digital Age
- Powers and Pitfalls of Facebook, Twitter, and Instagram
- WhatsApp Evolution and Digital Responsibility
- Impact of Digital Overload on Health and Society
- Freedom of Speech in a Diverse World
- Investment Guide for the Stock Market
- A Guide to Trading Shares, Commodities, Forex, and Cryptocurrencies
- Overcoming Smoking, Alcohol, and Drug Addiction
- Freedom from Addictions
- A Comprehensive Guide to Therapeutic Healing
- Navigating Challenges in Lower-Class Society
- A Guide to Road Safety and Accident Prevention
- Elderly Journeys: Life in Old Age Homes
- Breaking Free from the Fear of Society
- Challenges and Solutions in the Medical Field

- Challenges and Solutions for Adult Children
- A Guide to Estate Wills, Conflicts, and Resolutions
- Breaking Free from Debt
- Breaking Free from Domestic Violence
- A Comprehensive Guide to Women's Safety
- Modern Dating and Healthy Relationships
- Causes and Consequences of Extra-Marital Affairs
- Overcoming Jealousy and Leg-Pulling in Life
- Safeguarding from Blackmail and Online Threats
- Empowering Seniors in the Digital World
- Strategies to Overcome Office Challenges
- Life in Multinational Companies
- Challenges of the Middle Class
- A Guide to Divorce and Fresh Beginnings
- Navigating the World of Offline and Online Shopping
- Navigating Challenges in High Society
- Exploring the World of Online Reviews
- How Social Media Shapes Our Lives and Relationships?
- Entrepreneurship in the Digital Landscape
- A Guide to SEO Executive Skills
- Exploring the Dynamics of Online Messaging
- Safeguarding Against Crime in Everyday Life
- Challenges in IT and Digital Marketing
- Life and Challenges of IT Professionals
- Unveiling Common Life Struggles
- Navigating Student Life: Challenges and Solutions
- Soul Connections and Inner Discovery
- Overcoming Hurdles in Married Life
- A Guide to Managing Anxiety, Depression, and Stress
- Addressing Social Issues in India
- A Journey into Indian Mentality
- Resolving Conflicts in Relationships
- Reflections on the Dark Side of Human Nature
- Journalism Ethics and Challenges
- Women Entrepreneurs in the Modern World
- Choosing the Right Education and Career
- Choosing the Right Business for Financial Freedom

- Strategies for Overcoming Life's Challenges
- A Holistic Guide to Mental Health
- A Guide to Professional Challenges and Triumphs
- Everyday Wisdom: Small Tips for a Fulfilling Life
- Insights into Financial Frauds and Scams
- A Guide to Ethical Considerations in Various Professions
- Understanding and Overcoming LGBT Challenges
- Finding Happiness in Everyday Life
- Transform Your Life with Positive Affirmations
- Understanding and Managing Love Affairs
- Finding Purpose and Strength in Life's Challenges
- Understanding Financial Fraud's Impact on Victims
- Navigating Kundalini Awakening and Spiritual Growth
- Journey to Enlightenment: Wisdom from Spiritual Masters
- Artificial Intelligence and Its Transformative Impact on Society
- Avoiding Common Mistakes in the Modern World
- A Comprehensive Guide to Elderly Well-being
- Comprehensive Guide for IT Job Applicants: Key Questions and Answers
- Love Beyond Romance: Building a Strong and Lasting Marriage
- The Dark Side of Social Evils
- A Journey to Inner Peace and Enlightenment
- A Comprehensive Guide to Personal Transformation
- A Comprehensive Guide to Digital Marketing
- Techniques for Healing and Transforming Your Life

"Social Media Frauds and Online Scams" takes readers on a deep dive into the dark side of online platforms, exploring the alarming rise of fraud and scams through social media. From the early evolution of social media scams to sophisticated AI-driven deception and deepfake manipulations, this book uncovers the vulnerabilities that fraudsters exploit on platforms like Facebook, Instagram, and beyond. With real-world examples of phishing, romance scams, and influencer fraud, it equips readers with essential knowledge to protect themselves from the growing threats of online deception while offering practical strategies for prevention and recovery.

ABOUT THE AUTHOR

Mr. C. P. Kumar is a retired Scientist 'G' from National Institute of Hydrology, Roorkee, Uttarakhand, India. He is also a Reiki Healer and Chakra Balancing practitioner (with pendulum dowsing) and offers Emotional Freedom Technique (EFT) to help individuals with emotional issues. Mr. Kumar has authored many books on technical, spiritual, and social topics.

For further details, you may visit his webpage
https://www.angelfire.com/nh/cpkumar/virgo.html

www.ingramcontent.com/pod-product-compliance
Lightning Source LLC
Chambersburg PA
CBHW050258230526
45471CB00005B/1929